# See John Run

The Complete Radio 2
Janet & John Marsh Stories
As told by Terry Wogan

Kevin Joslin

**headline**

# For Alice and Tom

First published in 2009
by HEADLINE PUBLISHING GROUP

This edition published in 2010
by HEADLINE PUBLISHING GROUP

1

Cataloguing in Publication Data is available from the British Library

ISBN 978 0 7553 6170 0

Typeset in Plantin MT Schoolbook by
Avon DataSet Ltd, Bidford-on-Avon, Warwickshire

Printed and bound in Great Britain by Clays Ltd, St Ives plc

HEADLINE PUBLISHING GROUP
An Hachette UK Company
338 Euston Road
London NW1 3BH

www.headline.co.uk
www.hachette.co.uk

www.togs.org

# Flick the pages!
# See Janet beat up John!

# Contents

# Foreword
## by Sir Terry Wogan

Every time I stick my head above the parapet these days, I'm accosted by a little old lady who tells me how much she enjoys the Janet & John stories. Now, either little old ladies are still living in the world of 'naughty' boys and girls, like Just William and Violet Elizabeth Bott, or they've changed into salty old fishwives who turn the air blue at the Darby and Joan Club. A gnawing fear in my vitals tells me it's the latter . . . For there are no two ways about these earthy tales of a bearded eejit and his dominatrix wife. Not for the squeamish, nor the faint of heart, how they have escaped the BBC's infamous Programme Prevention Officer and made their dirty, double-meaning way over the airwaves and into the nation's heaving bosom is a mystery.

The plain people of Britain are regularly found weeping at the roadside, crying over their Wheaty-bangs, spraying the wallpaper with coffee or tea, frightening their fellow train passengers with hysterical shrieking or slumped at a desk, trails of mascara still wet on their cheeks, having heard these homely vignettes. And now, the *éminence grise* behind it all, the shadowy Kevin Joslin, gives us the works in print. Buy this book, for goodness' sake, and read away. Not in front of the children, of course. Little old ladies, that's a different story . . .

# *Introduction*

Thank you for buying this book. I remain astonished at the continued popularity of the Janet & John stories. Just when I thought they would sink into the sunset with Terry's retirement and the demise of *Wake up to Wogan*, they pop up again on *Weekend Wogan* where they even have a 'jingle'. (Do you like a jingle?)

There can be few people less deserving of a reputation as a foppish lothario than John Marsh. Both he and Janet are the sort of people that you wish lived next door. Janet is no more the violent harridan than John is a lisping popinjay, but as is so often the case with anything that Terry broadcasts on Radio 2, reality is temporarily suspended for the Brigadoon-like duration of the show when, (mostly) within the bounds of decency, anything goes.

It's this engaging lunacy that drew me to *Wake up to Wogan* in the first place. I used to be a dedicated Radio 4 *Today* man. A petulant squabble between politicians was how I normally started the day. One day in 1998 I picked up a hire-car and all of the preset channels were tuned to Radio 2, so I started listening.

Within a few weeks, I was not only hooked, but writing to the nation's favourite Irishman. It was the late, and much lamented, Pauly Walters who spotted the potential of the stories and encouraged me to write more. How could I also not thank Sir Terry, who is every bit as warm, friendly and funny in person as he is on air.

Despite having had several major limbs replaced, Terry still manages to put in an honest two hours a week at the coal-face – holidays permitting – and still reads the stories. Without him and dear old Pauly, I would probably have heeded the words of my old headmaster, who rather prophetically told me, 'You have a dirty mind boy and it will do you no good', and the stories would never have been written.

Kevin Joslin (aka Mick Sturbs)

Part One

– The Early Years

# Chinese New Year

Today, Janet and John are going to a Chinese New Year party.

John takes out his purple silk mandarin costume with a pillbox hat with gold trimmings. See Fu Manchu.

The party is being held at the local Chinese restaurant. The restaurant owner, Dicky Wang, meets them at the door.

'Hello Mr and Mrs Marsh,' says Mr Wang.

Mr Wang is from China. See the bicycles.

Janet says, 'Kong hee fat choi,' to Mr Wang.

Janet knows how to say 'Happy New Year' in

Cantonese. Clever Janet.

Mr Wang says, 'Thank you,' and shows Janet and John to their seats.

Do you like Chinese food? John does. See John dribble on the menu.

Janet tells John to wipe his beard. Cross Janet.

Janet says, 'What shall we order, John? It all looks very nice.'

John says, 'Let's have the set meal for four.'

Greedy John.

Soon Mr Wang comes back and takes their order.

Lots of other people are arriving and soon the food is served. John gobbles his food down. See the prawns and noodles in Janet's hair. Messy John.

Mr Wang brings some fortune cookies and some jasmine tea. Janet breaks open the cracker and looks at the paper inside.

Janet says, 'Oh look, I have a lucky rat on mine.'

John has a dragon and some Chinese writing on

his. John does not have any pockets, so he tucks it down his sock.

Soon it is time for the fireworks and the dragon dancing in the street. See John dance and skip and clap his hands, John likes fireworks.

Janet says to John, 'You'd better go to the little boys' room before we go home as you don't have your pull-ups on this evening.'

See John walk to the back of the restaurant. John sees Mrs Wang who works in the kitchen.

John says, 'It was lovely food this evening, thank you.'

Mrs Wang says, 'I see you put away the message in your cracker. It is called a *tsujiura*. Do you want to know what the message means?'

'Yes please,' says John.

John gets the message out of his sock and shows Mrs Wang.

Mrs Wang says, 'It means dragon who lives on the ground. It is very lucky for your wife. You have a very big meal this evening. You enjoy the food?

 You sure pack it in!'

'Yes, it was lovely, thank you,' says John.

When John gets back, Janet has already paid for the meal and it is time to go home.

Janet says, 'You were gone a long time. Did you have an accident?'

'No,' says John. 'I saw Mrs Wang at the back of the shop. She said that she'd seen me tuck my *tsujiura* in my sock earlier and wanted to have a quick look. She told me that it was just as well I'd shown her as it was "dragon on the ground" and that you were very lucky.'

See Janet light the fuse and push some firecrackers down John's trousers.

See John jump and hop.

Poor John.

# John Goes Car Racing

Today, Janet and John are going car racing.

See John put on sparkly red overalls with white sequins and patent-leather driving gloves.

John won a competition in the *Fop & Dandy Gazette* for a day racing cars at Snetterton. Do you know where Snetterton is? Janet does. Snetterton is in Norfolk. See Bernard Matthews.

It is a long drive to Norfolk. See John bouncing up and down in his safety seat, making car noises all the way there. When they arrive at the racetrack Janet says, 'I'm just going into the village to pick up some tablets for this headache and something for dinner on Sunday. I'll be back soon.'

John waves to Janet as she drives off.

John skips through the door of the racing school. The man on the desk says, 'Ah yes, Mr Marsh. We have Mrs Ruffle teaching you today. Go through the doors and you will see her. Mrs Ruffle is wearing blue overalls.'

'Hello Mr Marsh,' says Mrs Ruffle.

'Hello Mrs Ruffle,' says John.

What fun!

John says, 'Do you teach car racing all of the time?'

Mrs Ruffle says, 'No, I sometimes teach sailing on the coast but this is much better because I don't get caught up in the traffic at Fakenham.'

Mrs Ruffle leads John to the car. It is a very fast yellow one.

John says, 'Do you have any other cars as this one clashes with my overalls?'

Mrs Ruffle shakes her head. See John drive

around the racetrack very fast. There are lots of other cars on the track and John bumps into one of them but there is no damage.

Mrs Ruffle says, 'You are a very good driver, Mr Marsh, and you took that last right-hand bend very well with a great line to the finish, but you tend to drive a bit too fast in some places.'

Do you know where Pitlochry is? John does. See the points on John's driving licence.

Soon it is time to go. John gets out of the car and says thank you to Mrs Ruffle, then skips back to the car park to meet Janet.

'Hello John,' says Janet, 'sorry I'm late. I picked up a lovely fresh duck for Sunday lunch. Did you have a nice time?'

'Yes,' says John. 'Mrs Ruffle said that I had a very smooth lap but noticed a big bump in the middle after a quick right-hander. She said that she enjoyed her session with me even though I finished a bit too quickly – and she didn't have to

worry about Fakenham either.'

Do you know how to concuss someone with a fresh duck?

Janet does.

Poor John.

# The Spring Fete

Today, Janet and John are going to the spring fete on the village green.

John is very excited as there will be games and cakes and fizzy drinks. John likes fizzy drinks.

Janet says, 'If you don't hurry up we will be late.'

John is putting on a fur-lined cape, knee-boots and a yellow frilly shirt. When Janet manages to get John away from the mirror they walk down the lane to the village green. There are lots of stalls, some rides and a stage where people are singing and dancing.

'I want you to behave yourself today. Here is your pocket money. I'm going to the refreshment tent. I'll see you by the archery display in half an hour,' says Janet.

See John skip off to look at the stalls. John sees his friend Alan at the cake stall. Alan comes from Wealdstone. See the bollards. Alan is eating a big cake.

'Hello John,' says Alan.

See John brushing off the cake crumbs. Do you know what SlimFast is? Alan doesn't.

Alan and John decide to watch the singing. Alan wants to sing a song. Alan knows lots of songs and a special one about where a woodpecker lives.

John and Alan decide to sing a song together. They are a bit nervous because all the girls are watching. John wants to sing some opera but Alan says that it would be better to sing a popular song. Alan has a nice voice and powerful glasses.

They sing a song called 'Mrs
Robinson'.

Do you know what groupies are? Mrs Dennison from the knitting stall and Mrs Nicholas from the farmers' market do. See John blush. Paint John's face red.

Soon it is time for John to meet Janet. See John skip to the refreshment tent.

Janet says, 'Did you have a nice time?'

'Yes,' says John. 'I met Alan by the cake stall. Alan and I got up on the stage and did an act for the girls. I wanted to give them a sample of my *Magic Flute* but Alan was afraid that it might go over their heads so we pulled ourselves together and put everything we'd got into "Mrs Robinson".'

See Janet pick up a hundred-pound draw-weight longbow and a big sharp arrow.

Do you know what a head start is?

John does.

Run, John, run!

# John and the Vacuum Cleaner

Today, it has stopped raining for ten minutes, so Janet and John are in the garden.

John has put on his best gardening clothes – a pair of sparkly blue wellingtons with gold stars, pink satin overalls with zebra-stripe detailing on the pockets and a big floppy pink hat with a feather.

John is a dandy.

Janet says, 'Do you know where the edging shears are, John?'

See John shake his head, John does not know

what edging shears are.

Janet says, 'I remember. I loaned them to Mrs Edwards down the road, pop around and ask for them back please, John.'

John says, 'Can I take my pogo stick?'

'No,' says Janet, 'you know it always makes you feel sick when you bounce too much. Besides, how will you carry the shears on a pogo stick?'

Can you stick out your bottom lip and sulk? John can.

Janet says, 'Hurry up, John, otherwise I won't have time to bake any jam tarts this afternoon.'

See John run out of the gate. John likes jam tarts.

See John hop and skip along the road to Mrs Edwards' house.

See John ring the bell, 'ding-dong'.

Mrs Edwards takes a long time to come to the door.

'Sorry, John,' says Mrs Edwards, 'can I help you?'

'Yes,' says John. 'I've come to pick up the edging shears.'

'Of course,' says Mrs Edwards, 'I was going to pop them around later. Come through to the kitchen and I'll get them for you.'

Mrs Edwards says, 'I'm having trouble with my vacuum cleaner. It's not picking anything up at all and the floor is covered in fluff. Mr Edwards has gone out, so I wonder if you could have a look at it? I know you are very good with your hands.'

'Of course,' says John. 'I can see it is a wet and dry cleaner. We used to have one of those.'

Do you think 'Goblin' is a funny name for a vacuum cleaner?

See John take off the cover of the cleaner, remove the hose and the dust bag.

Do you know that you should always unplug anything electrical before you take it apart? John doesn't. Silly John.

See John get an electric shock.

See John's beard stand on end.

Mrs Edwards quickly pushes John away from the vacuum with her laundry tongs. Clever Mrs Edwards.

See Mr Edwards come through the front door.

'Are you all right, John?' says Mr Edwards.

'I think so,' says John, 'but the mother-of-pearl buttons on my overalls have melted.'

Mrs Edwards makes John a cup of tea and when he is feeling better gives him the shears to take home.

When John arrives home, Janet is making the pastry for the jam tarts.

'You were gone a long time,' says Janet, 'what have you been up to?'

See the warning signs.

'Well,' says John, 'I went round to see Mrs Edwards. When I arrived, she asked for my opinion on her Goblin. Mrs Edwards said that she never used to have any trouble picking up bits of fluff and thought it might be because her suction wasn't good enough. I had just taken the hose and bag out and got a bit of a shock as her husband turned up. Mrs Edwards had to pull me off with a pair of laundry tongs.'

Can you gnash your teeth?

Janet can.

See Janet pick up her marble rolling pin.

See John sprint down the garden path.

Run, John, run!

# At the Haberdasher's

Today, John is going to the haberdashery shop to get some gold braid for his new silk shorts.

Haberdashery is a funny word isn't it? Can you spell haberdashery? John can't.

Janet gives John the money for the gold braid and says, 'Be careful when you cross the road.'

'I will,' says John.

See John wave goodbye to Janet as he skips down the road.

John arrives at the shop and opens the door. 'Ding-a-ling' goes the bell.

'Hello John,' says Mr Brotherstone.

John says 'Hello' and rushes over to look at all the wonderful colours of cloth and thinks how nice it would be to have lots of lovely bright clothes.

John picks up some shiny gold braid and goes to pay at the counter. Mrs Self is already at the counter. Mrs Self is from Edinburgh. See the tattoo.

'Hello John,' says Mrs Self.

'Hello Mrs Self,' says John.

What fun!

Mrs Self is struggling with a big bag.

'Can I help you with that bag?' says John.

Kind John.

'Thank you,' says Mrs Self. 'I just bought a big bag of duck feathers as I'm making some pillows.'

Clever Mrs Self.

'I have a big floppy hat with feathers in it,' says John.

John is a fop and a dandy.

Mrs Self says, 'Duck down is the best kind of filling for pillows, much better than goose.'

While John is holding the bag, Mrs Self says, 'I was wondering if you have some open-weave embroidered silk at all?'

Mr Brotherstone says 'Yes' and shows Mrs Self a pretty blue cloth from the storeroom at the back of the shop. 'Please take the sample.'

John gives the bag of feathers back to Mrs Self, pays for his braid and waves goodbye.

See John skip home.

When John arrives, Janet is making some pastry. Do you like pastry? John does. See the elasticated waist.

Janet says, 'Did you get your gold braid?'

'Yes,' says John. 'And I saw Mrs Self in the shop. Mrs Self was looking for a good organza. So Mr Brotherstone helped her out with a nice sample. Mrs Self asked if I would hold her down while I waited for my turn. She said it was a really good

stuffing and much better than the goose she usually gets.'

See Janet pick up her birthday present.

Do you think that a marble rolling pin is a nice birthday present?

John doesn't.

See the big red lumps.

Poor John.

# John Goes to the Shops

Janet wants John to go to the shops.

Janet says, 'I'd like a copy of *Hello!* magazine, a pullet and something for your dessert.'

John says, 'Can I take my scooter?'

'No,' says Janet, 'you won't be able to carry the shopping on your scooter.'

See Janet pat John's head.

'Do you need a shopping list?' says Janet.

John says, 'I don't need a list for just three things. I can remember.'

Clever John.

See John skip down the road to the shops.

John has to remember what he needs to buy. As he hops along, he repeats, '*Hello!*, pullet, my pudding, *Hello!*, pullet, my pudding.'

Do you know how to cross the road?

The people that hear John do. See the funny looks.

When John gets to the shops, he gets a copy of *Hello!* magazine, a pullet and a spotted dick for pudding.

John likes spotted dick – count the calories.

John gets out the envelope with the money in it and queues up by the tills.

Mrs Bickerdyke is in front of John at the tills.

'Eh-up Fluffywhiskers,' says Mrs Bickerdyke.

Mrs Bickerdyke is from Yorkshire. See the dark satanic mills.

'Hello Mrs Bickerdyke,' says John.

Mrs Bickerdyke says, 'What do you have for lunch today, John?'

John passes his bag to Mrs Bickerdyke to show her.

Mrs Bickerdyke drops her bag on the floor.

John helps her to pick everything up. Kind John.

'Thank you, Fluffywhiskers,' says Mrs Bickerdyke.

See John pay for his shopping and skip home.

Janet meets John at the door.

'Did you get everything?' says Janet.

'Yes,' says John, 'and I helped Mrs Bickerdyke.'

Janet says, 'I thought I told you not to speak to that woman.'

John says, 'She only wanted to see my lunch.'

Janet is very cross. See the warning signs.

John says, 'Mrs Bickerdyke dropped everything by the tills. She held on to my bag and could see my spotted dick and pullet while she was on her hands and knees.'

Can you make your mouth look like a belly button?

Janet can.

See Janet fetch her rolling pin.

Run, John, run!

# A Visit to the Butcher's

Today, Janet and John are going to the butcher's shop.

Janet has to make sure John gets plenty of red meat otherwise he goes all floppy.

Outside the butcher's shop, Janet remembers that she has to buy some parcel tape from the post office.

Janet says, 'I'm going to the post office, John. If you wait here and keep out of mischief I'll buy you a sherbet fountain.'

See John smile.

Do you like sherbet fountains? John does.

Sometimes John can eat a whole one without coughing sherbet all over the furniture. Clever John.

While John is waiting, he stands outside the butcher's shop and watches through the window. Mrs Forrest, the butcher's wife, sees John outside and invites him in. Kind Mrs Forrest.

'Hello Mrs Forrest,' says John.

'Hello John,' says Mrs Forrest.

What fun!

Mrs Forrest says, 'Och, I've had a busy morning, John, I must have a sit-doon.'

Mrs Forrest is from Scotland. See the deep-fried *Daily Record*.

John says, 'Can I help behind the counter please?'

'That's very kind,' says Mrs Forrest. 'I've been on my feet all morning.'

See John looking at the sharp knives. John says, 'Can I cut up some meat like a proper butcher?'

Mrs Forrest says, 'As long as you are careful.

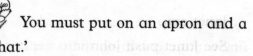

You must put on an apron and a hat.'

John is very careful and takes some bones out of a joint of meat, then cuts up some special steak for Mrs Wiseman.

Soon John sees Janet coming back to meet him, he thanks Mrs Forrest, washes his hands and runs out to meet Janet.

'Hello Janet,' says John.

'Hello John, did you behave yourself?' says Janet.

'Yes,' says John. 'Mrs Forrest invited me into the shop. She let me pretend to be the butcher's boy. She said that the way I handled the meat was remarkable, when it came to boning, she said I was a natural. Then I showed Mrs Wiseman how easily I could fillet. Can I have my sherbet fountain now?'

See Janet turn purple.

Can you make someone look like an Egyptian mummy with a roll of parcel tape?

Janet can.

See Janet push John into the boot of the car.

Poor John.

# The Hedge

Janet and John are in the garden. Janet wants to cut back the top of the hedge but can't reach. Poor Janet.

John can reach, see how tall John is, but John is not allowed to play with sharp things after the last time. See the plasters.

Janet sends John to borrow some long-handled shears from a neighbour.

Clever John remembers that he has often seen Mrs Frontage's gardener trimming her hedge. John rings the bell, 'ding-dong'.

'Hello Johnny,' says Mrs Frontage, 'what can I

do for you today?'

John says, 'I wondered if I could borrow some shears?'

'If you can find them,' says Mrs Frontage. 'I don't know what the gardener does with them. I have lots of hoes and rakes and things in the shed. Have a look in the tool chest.'

'Thank you,' says John.

See John looking in the tool chest.

Poor John. He can only find one pair of shears, and they are very old and rusty.

John goes next door to see Mr Terris. Mr Terris is not in, but Mrs Terris is.

Mrs Terris says, 'Charlie has some in the garage, let me help you find them.'

Kind Mrs Terris.

John thanks Mrs Terris, then takes the shears and goes home to Janet.

Janet says, 'You were gone a long time, what have you been up to?'

See the warning signs.

John says, 'I called in to see Mrs Frontage. She said that she could help me if I was looking for a hoe, but I could have a rummage about in her chest anyway. But I didn't find what I wanted. It wasn't until Mrs Terris showed me her Charlie's in the garage that I came across a decent pair. She also said that if I wanted to, I could pop around for secateurs any time.'

See Janet reach for her pruning knife.

See John make a big John-shaped hole in the hedge.

Run, John, run!

# Bonfire Night

John is very excited. See John skipping.

Janet dresses John in his best cardigan, his new balaclava, his duffel coat and his mittens on strings.

Janet holds John's hand all the way to the park because it is on a very busy road.

At the park there is a great big bonfire. Do you like bonfires?

John sometimes has a bonfire in his garden. See the neighbours get their washing in.

John has not had any tea, so Janet buys John a jumbo sausage.

Because John has been a good boy since 'the organ incident', Janet goes to buy John some ice cream.

John can't eat the sausage because he still has his mittens on.

See John waiting for the fireworks.

Silly John has forgotten to do something before he came out.

See John hopping about holding his sausage.

John needs to go to the little boys' room but he doesn't know what to do with his sausage.

See Mrs Bickerdyke.

'Eh-up Fluffywhiskers,' says Mrs Bickerdyke.

Mrs Bickerdyke is from Yorkshire. See the whippets.

John starts to cry. Poor John.

'What's the matter?' says Mrs Bickerdyke.

John sobs, 'I need to go to the little boys' room but I don't know what to do with my sausage.'

Mrs Bickerdyke takes the sausage and says, 'I'll look after it for you.'

Kind Mrs Bickerdyke.

John hops off to the little boys' room.

See John come back in a few minutes and take his sausage back.

'Thank you, Mrs Bickerdyke,' says John.

Janet sees John talking to Mrs Bickerdyke.

Janet doesn't like Mrs Bickerdyke. Janet is very cross.

Can you grind your teeth and hiss?

Janet can.

Janet shouts to John, 'Get over here this instant!'

John starts to cry again.

'What have I told you about talking to that woman?' says Janet.

John blubs, 'I needed to go to the little boys' room and I couldn't because of my mittens, so Mrs Bickerdyke held my sausage for me while I went.'

See the fireworks.

See Janet rub ice cream into John's beard.

Poor John.

# Janet and John Do the Gardening

Today, Janet and John are spring-cleaning the garden. Hear the birds sing.

John is helping Janet to dig the borders.

Janet says, 'Stop playing with worms and help me clear some of these weeds.'

See John empty his pockets.

Janet says, 'Can you help me pull up these weeds?'

See John shake his head, 'I'd like to help but my back is a bit sore.'

Do you know what a lazy fop is? Janet does.

'Go over the road to Mr Hall's and borrow something with a long handle, then you won't have to bend down,' says Janet.

Clever Janet.

See John ring the doorbell, 'ding-dong'. Mrs Hall comes to the door.

'Hello John,' says Mrs Hall. 'How can I help you?'

John says, 'I was wondering if I could borrow some of Charlie's gardening tools as I have a sore back and can't bend down?'

'Of course,' says Mrs Hall, 'come through to the shed.'

John likes sheds.

'I think he has just the thing, I've seen him using one before,' says John.

'If you don't mind I'll carry on with my gardening while you look,' says Mrs Hall. 'I've got a bit of trouble finding a climber I put in last year. I asked Charlie to have a look on Saturday, but he couldn't see it. Typical man.'

John soon finds what he is looking for and skips down the garden to see Mrs Hall.

'I've found some, thank you, Mrs Hall,' says John.

'Good,' says Mrs Hall. 'I planted a clematis vitalba behind this wall somewhere last year and it's got lost in all this ivy. Can you help me look for it?'

'Of course,' says John.

See John pulling up the ivy. Helpful John. John washes his hands and takes the tools back to Janet. Janet is putting in some canes for the sweet peas.

Janet says, 'You were gone a long time.'

'Yes,' says John. 'Mrs Hall said that I was probably looking for a hoe. I told her I'd been admiring her Charlie's for some time, so she let me see them in the shed. They were quite long but a good weight and nice to handle. Then I helped her trim back the undergrowth around her clematis as

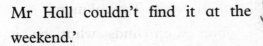

Mr Hall couldn't find it at the weekend.'

See Janet select a long, whippy cane.

Can you hurdle four-foot garden fences?

John can.

Run, John, run!

# The Steam Train

Today, Janet and John are going to have a ride on a steam train.

John is very excited. See John put on his puce Versace overalls and leather cap.

While Janet is driving to the station, John is bouncing up and down in his seat making train noises. Can you make train noises? Neither can John.

At the train station, Janet goes to get a cup of tea and some Tizer for John.

John sees Mrs Bickerdyke.

'Eh-up Fluffywhiskers,' says Mrs Bickerdyke.

Mrs Bickerdyke is from Yorkshire.
See Geoffrey Boycott.

Mrs Bickerdyke says, 'Are you driving the train today then, Johnny?'

John shakes his head sadly.

Mrs Bickerdyke says, 'Let me have a word with t' driver, I used to fettle his throckle through t' grate when he were a lad.'

See John look confused.

See Mrs Bickerdyke talking to the train driver.

Mrs Bickerdyke says, 'I've sorted it so that you can ride with the driver.'

'Thank you, Mrs Bickerdyke,' says John.

Soon Janet comes back with the drinks. John quickly gulps down his drink and tells Janet that he is going to ride with the driver.

'In that case,' says Janet, 'I'll stay here in the craft shop.'

Sensible Janet. See John climb up next to the train driver.

Mr Moncrieff, the driver, says, 'We have

 another helper today. This is Mrs Perkins from the post office.'

See John smile at Mrs Perkins.

Soon it is time to start the train. See John and Mrs Perkins shovel coal into the engine. See the hot flames and the steam. Mrs Perkins soon has to take off her cardigan.

Mr Moncrieff stops the train to pick up another carriage and shows John and Mrs Perkins how to attach it to the train. Mr Moncrieff lets Mrs Perkins sound the whistle three times as they go into a tunnel. What fun! See John taking photographs with Mrs Perkins' camera.

Soon the train journey is over. John thanks Mr Moncrieff and jumps down from the train to find Janet. John sees Janet buying a croquet set. Do you know how to play croquet? Janet does.

'Hello Janet,' says John. 'I had a lovely time on the train.'

'Did you?' says Janet.

John says, 'It got ever so hot so Mrs Perkins had

to take off some clothes. We worked up quite a head of steam so Mr Moncrieff watched us when we pulled into the sidings and coupled, then I took some photographs when Mrs Perkins pulled his whistle three times on the way home.'

See Janet staple John to the lawn with croquet hoops.

Do you know what a powerful backswing is?

Janet does.

Poor John.

# Janet and John Go for a Walk

Today, Janet and John are going out for a walk.

John puts on his cerise duffel coat with frogging on the sleeves and gold toggles, and his best gold-lamé bobble hat and gloves on strings.

Do you know what a fop is? Janet does.

As they walk down the lane, Janet sees Mr McWilliams, the builder.

'Hello Mr McWilliams,' says Janet.

'Hello Mrs Marsh,' says Mr McWilliams.

Mr McWilliams says, 'I'm just here to have a look at one of our new buildings.'

John says, 'Can I have a look at the building site please?'

Mr McWilliams says, 'Yes, of course, but you'll have to see Mrs Gough in the site office over there.'

See Mr McWilliams point at a big shed.

John likes big sheds.

Janet says, 'I'll go and have a cup of tea at the café and I'll see you back here in half an hour.'

See John trot over to the big shed. John is very excited.

When John goes into the big shed, he sees Mrs Gough behind the desk.

Mrs Gough says, 'Hello, John, what can I do for you this morning?'

John says, 'Mr McWilliams said I could have a look around the building site.'

'All right, John,' says Mrs Gough, 'but we'll have to make sure you're safe, enjoy the tour and have the right protection. Let me measure you up for a hard hat.'

See Mrs Gough measure John's head with a

tape measure. Do you know what a tape measure is? John has quite a big head!

Mrs Gough puts the hard hat on John's head and they go out to the building site. Mrs Gough shows John all of the big machines and the concrete mixer. Then they wait for a truck to deliver the tarmac for making driveways. See the big red truck.

'The truck is delivering what we call asphalt,' says Mrs Gough. 'I have to tell the man where I'd like him to put it.'

What fun!

Then they go back to the shed and have a cup of tea and a bacon sandwich at the kitchen table.

Do you like bacon sandwiches? John does. See the sauce in John's beard.

Soon John sees Janet coming back to the building site. John waves goodbye to Mrs Gough and Mr McWilliams and runs out to meet her by the concrete mixer.

'Hello Janet,' says John.

'Hello John,' says Janet. 'Did you enjoy yourself?'

'Oh yes,' says John. 'First, I went into the shed, and Mrs Gough said that if we were going to relax and enjoy ourselves, I'd need some protection, so she measured me up. Mrs Gough had a little trouble finding a good fit, because I'm a seven and a quarter, then she showed me where she wanted her asphalt and then took me back to the shed for something hot on the kitchen table.'

Can you make your lips disappear?

Janet can.

See Janet push John into the concrete mixer.

See John go round and round.

Poor John.

# A Trip to the Supermarket

Today, Janet and John are going to the shops.

It is raining this morning so John puts on a silver and blue waterproof poncho with white tassels and bright yellow cowboy boots with stars on them.

When they get to the shops John says, 'Please can I go to the soft-play area?'

Janet says, 'No,' and pulls John's reins.

See John lay on the ground and hold his breath.

After Janet has dried John's tears, they go to the supermarket.

John says, 'Can I go and read the comics please?'

Janet says, 'Yes, but no top-shelf books.'

Do you like books about shelves? John does.

While John is reading the October edition of *Mighty Organs*, someone taps him on the shoulder.

'Hello John,' says Mrs Hersey.

'Hello Mrs Hersey,' says John.

Mrs Hersey says, 'I was just in here looking for my bridge magazine. We often make up a four with Mr and Mrs Ratcliff or Mr and Mrs Geddis from down the road.'

'I like playing card games,' says John. 'My favourites are old maid and happy families.'

Mrs Hersey says, 'Have you ever played bridge?'

'No,' says John. 'Mostly I watch the television in my shed in the evenings or play on my organ.'

'We never bother with the television these days,' says Mrs Hersey. 'Mr Hersey prefers to switch it off. Why don't you and Janet come over and we'll teach you to play? We can sit Mr Hersey with Janet and I can sit with you while you learn.'

Kind Mrs Hersey explains to John all about how to play bridge.

'Thank you, Mrs Hersey,' says John.

Soon Janet comes back with the shopping in a big trolley.

'Hello Janet,' says John.

Janet says, 'Who was that lady I saw you talking to?'

John says, 'That was Mrs Hersey, she was telling me all about a game she and her husband play with other couples from their road in the evenings. Mrs Hersey says that we should join them for supper and a few games. They don't bother with television and most evenings have it off. She said that Mr Hersey would be happy to teach you what to do and said that they usually manage to get through at least four rubbers.'

Do you know how to ruin a perfectly good umbrella?

Janet does.

Hear the screams.

Poor John.

# In the Bath

John is in the bath. See the bubbles. Splish-splash.

Janet has gone to the shops to buy some salad. Do you like salad? John does.

There is someone at the door. Hear the doorbell, 'ding-dong'.

Hear John say some rude words. Do you know any rude words? John knows lots.

See John run down the stairs and open the door in his bathrobe. Why do you think John has a door in his bathrobe?

See Mrs Dix, the postlady, at the door.

'Hello Mr Marsh,' says Mrs Dix.

'Hello Mrs Dix,' says John.

Mrs Dix says, 'I have a parcel for you, Mr Marsh, is it one of your special video films about people who have lost all their clothes?'

See John blush. Paint John's cheeks red.

'No,' says John, 'it is some organ music I have been waiting for.'

Mrs Dix says, 'Is that your organ I can see, the big shiny one?'

'Yes,' says John, 'it's a seven-stop, two-manual 1938 Woodstock pipe organ but I can't use it at the moment as pumping it makes Janet's arm ache.'

'I could pump it for you,' says Mrs Dix.

Kind Mrs Dix.

'That would be lovely,' says John, 'but you have to pump quite hard to get it started as my bellows are rather old and perished.'

See Mrs Dix pumping. Pump-pump-pump. John's friend Paul knows a song about that.

Hear John play Bach's Prelude and Fugue in D major. Clever John.

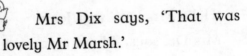

Mrs Dix says, 'That was lovely Mr Marsh.'

See John blush again.

See Janet arrive home.

'Hello Mrs Marsh,' puffs Mrs Dix. 'Mr Marsh was showing me the organ in his bathrobe. He can do some wonderful things with it, even though he is out of practice.'

Can you swoop down like a wolf on the fold?

Janet can.

See Janet get a big green cucumber out of her bag.

Are you sitting comfortably?

John isn't.

# John Goes Carol Singing

John is going out carol singing with his friend Pauly.

It is very cold. John puts on his duffel coat and woolly hat.

John and Pauly crunch up the drive to the first big house and knock on the door.

What fun!

Mrs Frontage answers the door.

Mrs Frontage owns a shop in the village with blacked-out windows called 'Private Shop'.

John sometimes spends all his pocket money in her shop.

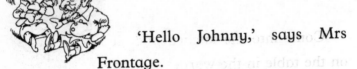

'Hello Johnny,' says Mrs Frontage.

'Hello Mrs Frontage,' say Pauly and John.

Mrs Frontage says, 'Please, call me Melanie. Pauly's a big boy for his age isn't he?'

Do you know what a trollop is when you see one? Pauly does.

Hear John and Pauly sing 'Hark the Herald Angels'.

'Would you boys like to come in for a special treat?' says Mrs Frontage.

'Yes please!' say Pauly and John.

Mrs Frontage gets out two enormous wobbly pink blancmanges and gives the boys one each.

'Thank you very much,' say John and Pauly. 'We've never had these before.'

The next house they come to belongs to Mr Ruffley.

'Ding-dong' goes the bell.

Mr Ruffley is not in. Mrs Ruffley calls to the boys to come to the back door.

'Come into the kitchen and sit on the table in the warm,' says Mrs Ruffley.

Kind Mrs Ruffley.

The boys sit on the table and sing 'We Three Kings'.

Mrs Ruffley gives them each a shiny fifty-pence piece.

It is nearly eight o'clock and time to go home. John waves goodbye to Pauly.

Pauly seems to be going back to see Melanie Frontage for seconds.

John goes home to Janet.

'Did you have a nice time?' asks Janet.

John says, 'Yes. Mrs Frontage let us try out her big pink jellywobblers, and at number 41 we entertained the present Mrs Ruffley on the kitchen table while her husband was out.'

See Janet tap the barometer.

Janet is tapping the barometer with John's head.

Poor John.

# The Christmas Fair

Today, Janet and John are going to the Christmas fair in the village hall.

John is very excited.

At the hall there are lots of stalls selling sweets, cakes and home-made jam.

See Janet give John his pocket money.

Janet says, 'Don't spend it all on sweets, John.'

Janet goes off to look for a toasting fork.

John walks around the stalls.

John sees Melanie Frontage, who sells helpful equipment for when you get married.

Today, Mrs Frontage is dressed all in pink.

John's friend Pauly knows a song about that.

See John avoiding Mrs Frontage's stall.

Do you know what happened last time? Janet does. So does John. See the bruises.

John sees a stall with lots of cakes.

Do you like cakes? John does.

See John looking for some gateau. Do you know what a gateau is?

'Excuse me, Mrs Wiseman,' says John, 'do you have any gateau please?'

'Yes,' says Mrs Wiseman. 'I have a big Black Forest gateau, but there wasn't room on the stall. It's under the table. Would you like some?'

John says, 'Yes please.'

Mrs Wiseman says, 'Lift up the tablecloth and cut yourself a big slice. My husband isn't looking so you can have it for free.'

Kind Mrs Wiseman.

John thanks Mrs Wiseman for the gateau, which he gobbles down.

John sees Janet coming back.

'Have you spent your pocket money yet?' says Janet.

See John shake his head.

'Good boy,' says Janet. 'What have you been doing?'

John says, 'I was looking at the cake stall for some gateau and Mrs Wiseman said that if I looked under the tablecloth I'd see her Black Forest. She told me to help myself as her husband wasn't looking.'

See Janet get out her new toasting fork.

See John run.

Run, John, run!

# Piano Lessons

Today, Janet and John are going into the town to do some shopping.

John puts on his mauve crushed-velvet morning coat, aquamarine top hat and gold waistcoat.

As soon as Janet can get John away from the full-length mirror in the hall, they set off for the bus stop.

Janet says, 'Remember, John, you have already spent all of your pocket money this week on an Elizabethan ruff, so unless you get a part-time job soon, there will be no sweets for you.'

See John's lip tremble. Poor John.

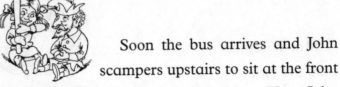

Soon the bus arrives and John scampers upstairs to sit at the front where he can pretend to be the driver. Hear John making bus noises. Do you know what an embarrassment is? Janet does.

When the bus arrives in town, Janet says to John, 'You can go and look at the shops while I go to the Co-op to pick up a new frying pan. I will see you back here in half an hour.'

See John wave to Janet as he skips off down the road. There are so many shops. There are shoe shops, a charity shop, more shoe shops and another charity shop, and there's an estate agent. John goes into a charity shop.

John is looking at some of the books when he sees Mrs Wiseman.

'Hello John,' says Mrs Wiseman. 'Are you shopping today?'

John says, 'I'm only looking because I've spent all my pocket money and can't have any more until I get a part-time job.'

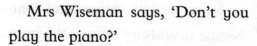

Mrs Wiseman says, 'Don't you play the piano?'

'Yes,' says John, 'I have one at home.'

Mrs Wiseman says, 'Why don't you give piano lessons? I'd pay you. I used to get lessons from Mrs Beedo at the school, but she's quite a cross lady. Do you know her?'

'Yes,' says John, 'I have known Lola for a long time and she is rather cross.'

Mrs Wiseman says, 'Well perhaps I could come to your house for lessons? Is ten pounds an hour all right?'

See John smile.

'Yes,' says John. 'Wednesday would be a good day because Janet is out on Wednesdays and she doesn't like the noise.'

Kind John.

'I'll see you then,' says Mrs Wiseman.

Soon it is time for John to meet Janet. See John skip along the road. See John wave to Janet. What fun!

Janet says, 'I hope you have been a good boy.'

'Yes,' says John, 'and I have a part-time job too!'

Janet says, 'Clever boy! Is it a paper round?'

John says, 'No, I saw Mrs Wiseman, she said I would be perfect for what she needs because she used to have problems with Lola Beedo but now she can come round every Wednesday while you're out and have a go on my old upright for ten pounds an hour.'

Do you know how to ruin a perfectly good non-stick surface?

Janet does.

See Janet chase John.

Run, John, run!

# John Plays the
# Church Organ

This evening, John is going to play the church organ.

John likes playing the organ.

'It's quite cold outside,' says Janet, 'so make sure you wrap up.'

John puts on his knee-length, pink leather boots, a gold lamé balaclava and his best purple fur coat. See Roo Paul.

It is quite dark when John gets to the church. John is not afraid of the dark. Brave John.

Mrs Casey is already at the church arranging

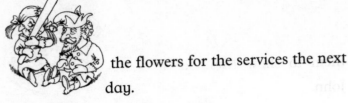 the flowers for the services the next day.

'Hello Mrs Casey,' says John.

'Hello John,' says Mrs Casey.

What fun!

John gets out his music and sits down at the organ and begins to play.

Do you know how to play Bach's Prelude and Fugue in B minor? John does. Clever John.

Mrs Casey says, 'That was wonderful, John. I've just noticed that there are some vase holders on both sides of the organ where I could put some flowers.'

John likes flowers.

'I'll go and ask the new pastor if that would be all right.'

'That's a good idea,' says John. 'I haven't met the new pastor yet either.'

While Mrs Casey is away, John looks in one of the cupboards where some of the music is kept. John sees the vases that fit the organ and takes

them to show Mrs Casey. Kind John.

Mrs Casey is in the vestry with the new pastor, Mr Kidneys. See John knock on the door. Mr Kidneys opens the door and introduces himself to John.

'Mrs Casey will be with you shortly,' he says. 'She's just under the sink looking for some more vases. Was that you playing the organ earlier? I recognised the Bach, but what was the second piece?'

John says, 'That was "Prayer and Alleluias" from *Three Pieces for Organ* by Calvin Hampton.'

'I liked that a lot,' says Pastor Kidneys, 'so did Mrs Casey, please play some more.'

Soon Mrs Casey comes back and sees the vases. 'Thank you, John,' she says. 'I'll have to see what autumn flowers I can find to put in them. Of course it's much better in the spring. I have lovely red and yellow tulips in my garden that would make a beautiful display. My husband is always away in springtime so I have lots of time to pick the best flowers.'

John and the pastor watch Mrs Casey arranging her flowers, then John plays some more on the organ.

Soon it is time for John to leave. See John wave goodbye to Pastor Kidneys and Mrs Casey.

When John gets home, Janet is knitting. Janet likes knitting.

Janet says, 'Did you have a nice time, John?'

'Yes I did,' says John. 'I played for quite a long time on the organ; then I was helping Mrs Casey who was in the vestry. When I knocked on the vestry door Mrs Casey was on her knees and the man said he was Pastor Kidneys. He said Mrs Casey would be happy to deal with me next. She was very impressed with the Hampton. Even the pastor said it was a fine piece. Mrs Casey said that she can't wait for the spring when her husband is away and she can get her tulips around that organ.'

See Janet get out her Denise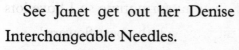
Interchangeable Needles.

Can you make someone look like a hedgehog?

Janet can.

Hear the screams.

Poor John.

# John Goes to the Chemist's

Today, John is going to the chemist's. John goes to the chemist's every Monday to get his blue pills.

See John put on a dark-grey suit and an old duffel coat so no one will recognise him. Clever John.

Janet says, 'While you are at the chemist's, remember to pick up those photographs and something for lunch, but don't go buying any more comics and sweets as you don't get your pocket money until Wednesday.'

See Janet give John a list of the things he has to

remember with the money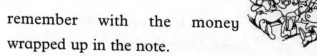
wrapped up in the note.

See John skip down the road to the bus stop. It is quite cold this morning and John has forgotten his mittens on strings. Silly John.

John catches the bus into the village and gets off at the stop near the chemist's.

Mrs Reddington sees John come into the shop. 'Hello John,' she says, 'is it time for your pills again already?'

See John blush.

'Yes,' says John, 'and I wanted to pick up some photographs we were having developed too.'

Mrs Reddington says, 'As long as it's not the newsreaders' wives ones again.'

See John blush again. Paint John's face red.

'I have them right here,' says Mrs Reddington. 'I just got mine back from my holiday too.'

John says, 'Where did you go?'

Mrs Reddington says, 'We went to Freiburg in Germany. Look, here's a picture of me buying a great big sausage with our tour guide, Herr Grubers.'

John says, 'His head looks very red.'

Mrs Reddington laughs, 'Yes, it was very hot and Herr Grubers had no hair so I had to rub some suncream in to stop him burning.'

What fun!

John pays Mrs Reddington for the blue pills and the photographs and hops and skips over the road to the supermarket to get some lunch. John goes to the hot counter. There are lots of nice things cooking on the grills. Chickens, sausages and spare ribs.

While John is deciding what to buy he sees Mrs Bickerdyke.

'Eh-up Fluffywhiskers,' says Mrs Bickerdyke.

Mrs Bickerdyke is from Yorkshire. See the ridiculous terriers.

Mrs Bickerdyke says, 'Those pork joints look grand. I might have one of them with some new potatoes and garden peas.'

'Oh yes,' says John, 'that sounds very nice.'

See John buy a pork joint too.

Mrs Bickerdyke says, 'Have you come on the bus today?'

See John nod his head.

Mrs Bickerdyke says, 'I'll give thee a lift home.'

Kind Mrs Bickerdyke.

On the way home, Mrs Bickerdyke lets John have some of the spare crackling from her roast pork.

When John gets in, Janet is in the kitchen loading the dishwasher.

Janet says, 'Did you remember to get the photographs and some lunch?'

'Yes,' says John. 'Mrs Reddington showed me some photographs of her getting a big sausage in the Black Forest. It was so hot and sweaty that she had to rub some cream into Herr Grubers to prevent burning. Then I saw Mrs Bickerdyke in the supermarket. She was after something hot at lunchtime and let me have a bit of crackling in the car on the way home.'

See Janet push John into the dishwasher and shut the door.

Poor John.

# Janet and John
# Go to an Auction

Today, Janet and John are going to an auction.

Do you know what an auction is?

An auction is a place where people sell old things that they don't want to keep.

Janet says, 'I wonder how much we could get for you, John?'

Funny Janet!

John is dressed in a pink velvet catsuit with silver knee-length boots, a silver belt and matching cape.

Do you think John looks like an oven-ready turkey? Janet does.

The auction is being held in the village hall.

When Janet and John arrive, they see Pastor Kidneys.

'Hello Janet and John,' says Pastor Kidneys, 'have you come to buy something for the house?'

Janet says, 'No, we're just looking today, but if something nice comes up we might be interested. By the way, do you still want me to post some leaflets about the summer fete?'

'Yes please,' says Pastor Kidneys. 'Would you like to come up to the church and pick some up? There are some posters and drawing pins too if you'd like them and Mrs Kidneys has made you a big bowl of trifle to say thank you.'

Do you like trifle? John does.

Janet says, 'Be a good boy while I'm gone, I'll see you back here by the noticeboard – and don't buy anything at the auction!'

'I won't,' says John.

While he is waiting, John decides to walk

around the auction and look at all of the things that are for sale. There is a wardrobe with a mirror, a dressing table and a big chest.

'Eh-up Fluffywhiskers,' says Mrs Bickerdyke.

Mrs Bickerdyke is from Yorkshire. See Arthur Scargill.

'I didn't know you liked furniture,' says Mrs Bickerdyke. 'I'm down here all the time buying new bits for the house. I'm after a tallboy for the bedroom now. Only last week I bought a lovely white, painted, Shaker-style chest and a matching chest of drawers. It looks lovely in front of the big mirror. Now, you're good with your hands aren't you? A couple of the drawers need a bit taken off of them so that they don't stick and the lock on the chest needs replacing. Be a good boy and pop around with your toolbox and I'll see you all right.'

Do you know how to get a word in edgeways? John doesn't.

Soon Janet is back from the church with the leaflets and posters.

'Who was that I saw you talking to?' says Janet.

See the warning signs.

John says, 'That was Mrs Bickerdyke. She was looking for a tallboy today. She said she had some things that I can do for her in return for money and said I'll have to come round and see her Shaker chest in the bedroom and dresser with tight drawers in front of the big mirror. Can I have some trifle now?'

See Janet tip the bowl of trifle down John's trousers and pin him to the noticeboard.

Poor John.

Part Two
– The Middle Years

# John Goes to the
# Dry-cleaner's

Today, Janet and John are going to the dry-cleaner's.

John has a lot of dry-cleaning as all of his clothes are made of satin, silk and lace. John is a popinjay.

John is wearing his new summer outfit: purple gumboots, waterproof pink trousers and a silver sou'wester with orange stars. As soon as John has been strapped into the safety seat, Janet drives into town. Janet parks behind the dry-cleaner's and John helps her to carry all the dry-cleaning into

 the shop. See Janet and John queue up at the counter.

'Can I go and play outside?' says John.

Janet says, 'Yes, but stay out of mischief if you can.'

'I will,' says John.

John walks down the street and looks in the shop windows. John likes shopping. See the credit-card bills. John sees Mrs Joy. John remembers that Mrs Joy used to work in the post office in the 1970s. Do you remember the 1970s? John does. See John dance 'The Hustle'.

'Hello Mrs Joy,' says John.

'Hello John,' says Mrs Joy.

What fun!

Mrs Joy says, 'I only came into town to pick up a big new gun bag from Mr Bentley. We do a lot of shooting.'

John says, 'I hope you don't shoot cute bunny rabbits.'

'No,' says Mrs Joy, 'we go target shooting.'

John says, 'Isn't that rather dangerous?'

Mrs Joy laughs and says, 'No, we are well out of the way of danger even when we are marking the shots at the end of the range. There is a big bank of earth in front of the targets and a ditch behind in which the markers sit, raise and lower the targets, and point out where the shots have hit. It's called the butts. We usually split into two teams, men and ladies. The ladies don't mind taking time to mark the shots as they don't have to wear ear protectors, which mess up their hair. If you like, you could come along to the open day at Bisley in September. I'd be happy to take you along.'

Kind Mrs Joy.

John wonders if you can get sparkly, green waxed cotton.

'Yes please,' says John.

John says goodbye to Mrs Joy and hops and skips back to the dry-cleaner's to meet Janet.

Janet is just paying for the dry-cleaning and getting some new suit covers.

'Did you behave?' says Janet.

John says, 'Yes, I saw Mrs Joy. She came into town to see Mr Bentley who has a big bag for her. Mrs Joy was telling me all about what she gets up to out in the country at the weekends. You need a special licence from the police and a half decent weapon. They normally have a team of men and ladies, and everyone has a chance to score. She said that most of the ladies don't mind it in the butts, as they don't need protection from all the banging. She said if I'd like to give it a try, she'd be happy to take me out.'

Can you force a whole newsreader into a zip-up suit cover?

Janet can.

See John's face go blue through the little plastic window.

Poor John.

# The Nursery

Today, Janet and John are going to the plant nursery.

Do you know what a plant nursery is? John doesn't.

See John put on his best play clothes. Bright yellow dungarees, a red and white stripy jumper and a bright orange baseball cap with sequins. See Timmy Mallett.

'No, John,' says Janet, 'it's not the right day for your playgroup, we are going to the plant nursery.'

See John hold his breath and lay on the floor. Paint John's face purple.

John is very cross and it takes ages to get him strapped into his safety seat. Naughty John. When they arrive at the nursery, there are lots of people buying plants for the garden. See the Volvos.

Janet says, 'I'm going to look for some cacti and something for the hanging baskets. Can I trust you not to get into mischief?'

'Yes,' says John. 'I will be a very good boy.'

While John is waiting, he goes to look at some of the vegetable plants in the big greenhouse.

'Hello,' says Mrs Higgins. 'Were you looking for something special?'

'No,' says John. 'But I always wanted to grow the really big vegetables that win prizes.'

John likes prizes.

Mrs Higgins says, 'The easiest prize plants to grow are usually the marrows or pumpkins. They can get to be enormous, but you have to make sure that they get plenty of water and are fed regularly if you want very large specimens. If you go into

the shop, you can see photographs
of some of the prize vegetables I have
grown.'

Clever Mrs Higgins.

'Can I buy some of the plants to grow great big
vegetables?' says John.

'Of course,' says Mrs Higgins. 'Marrows are
always very popular at the Women's Institute
garden show, I can let you have two marrow
plants for the price of one if you are interested.'

'Yes please,' says John.

Mrs Higgins says, 'Let me know when you are
going to plant them as they need to be covered up
with plastic to start with until they get used to
being outside. You should fertilize the soil before
you plant them and prick them out about two feet
apart otherwise they will get too crowded. Don't
worry too much about top-dressing them until
they are a bit bigger. I can pop around to give you
a hand if you like?'

Kind Mrs Higgins.

See John hop and skip over to the shop to look at the photographs of really big vegetables.

Soon, John sees Janet.

'Hello Janet,' says John.

Janet says, 'Have you been a good boy?'

'Yes,' says John. 'Mrs Higgins was telling me all about her prize-winning specimens. She said that she thought I could win prizes too as long as I make sure that I have a well-prepared bed. She wants to come around and see me prick out two feet apart, and to make sure I have proper protection while hardening off. She told me not to worry about dressing before she comes round and said that in no time at all I could have something that would be worth showing to the Women's Institute.'

Do you know how many cacti Janet can force down John's dungarees?

John does.

Hear the screams.

Poor John.

# John Goes Bell-ringing

Today, John is going to play the church organ.

John likes playing the organ. See John's thick glasses. John puts on his special church clothes: an orange cassock with pink sequins, knee-length, blue, patent-leather boots and a gold archbishop's mitre.

See Janet roll her eyes.

When John arrives at the church, he puts his scooter up against the railings and gets out the organ music from his handbag.

John sees Pastor Kidneys.

'Hello Pastor Kidneys,' says John.

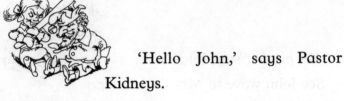

'Hello John,' says Pastor Kidneys.

What fun!

Pastor Kidneys is going into town. He says, 'I know you've come to practise the organ today, John, but the ladies are also here to do some bell-ringing. I hope that you don't mind the noise. Some people don't like it at all.'

See the angry letters.

John says, 'Actually, I rather enjoy it.'

John hops and skips into the church and is about to sit down at the organ when he sees Melanie Frontage.

'Hello Johnny,' says Melanie Frontage.

Melanie Frontage has a private shop with dark windows.

See everything.

Melanie Frontage says, 'I'm here with the other ladies to practise our bell-ringing, but we're one short and we want to try ringing a carillon. Could you help out?'

'Yes please,' says John.

See John wave to Mrs Dickins and Mrs Forrest from the village.

Melanie Frontage says, 'All you have to do is to stand here and follow what we do. You take hold of the bell rope by the woollen grip, called the sally, and when you pull down, you must let go of the top of the rope and catch the bottom of the sally before you can pull it again. The bells in English churches swing on something called the headstock. On the continent, the bells don't move as much.'

See John watch what the ladies do, and when it is his turn he pulls down very hard on the rope.

'Ding-dong' go the bells.

'Not too hard,' says Mrs Dickins, 'otherwise the rope will come away from the bell and you'd have to climb up to fix it.'

'That is called ringing in the round,' says Mrs Forrest. 'Next we will ring to a pattern called ringing the changes.'

See John pulling on the bell rope.

John likes ringing the bells.

Soon it is time to go home. John unchains his scooter and races along the road.

When John gets home, Janet is oiling her cricket bat.

'Hello John,' says Janet. 'Did you have a good practice?'

John says, 'No, I didn't have time. I saw Melanie Frontage, Mrs Forrest and Mrs Dickins from the village. They asked if I would like to join them for a carillon. After I'd done the rounds I was quite tired and had to have a rest before we could ring the changes. Melanie Frontage said that they do it differently at our churches as, unlike the continent, they swing freely. She said I had a good strong handstroke, but Mrs Dickins said I need to be careful not to pull too hard in case the end came off.'

See Janet go purple.

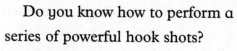

Do you know how to perform a
series of powerful hook shots?
Janet does.
Poor John.

# John Goes to Work

Today, John is going to work.

John has a part-time job, but sometimes gets work on the side that Janet doesn't know about. Do you know what a brown envelope is? John does. Clever John.

John puts on his special work clothes – a pink doublet and hose with pale-green trimmings and a big, feathered hat.

John is a fop and a dandy.

Janet says, 'Try not to be too late as we're having shish kebabs for dinner.'

John likes shish kebabs. See the facial scars.

John goes to his job as a junior traffic-boy at the BBC then goes off to present an award.

The award is for the best manicurist in the country. John likes manicures. Do not see the cuticles.

When John arrives, the guests at the award are just having something to eat.

See John push in at the front of the queue for the buffet. Naughty John.

John has already eaten half a chicken, three Scotch eggs and a plate of sausages and is just starting on a big slice of seed cake when the award is announced.

See John get up on stage, still eating his cake. Greedy John.

See John give the lady who has won two big silver trophies and some pearls and kiss her on the cheek. See the cake crumbs.

There are lots of people taking photographs. Do you like being photographed? John does. See John elbow the lady to one side.

After the award, John collects his money and buys lots of sweets and comics before he catches the train.

When John arrives home, Janet is just finishing the kebabs.

'Did you have a nice day at work, John?' says Janet.

'Nothing special,' says John, as he puts down his bag.

See the brown envelope fall out of John's handbag.

Janet says, 'Where did that money come from? The BBC doesn't pay you in brown envelopes.'

John says, 'I managed to get something on the side today. I had to get up on stage with a nice lady while some men took photographs. She had an enormous pair of cups. I had to kiss her on the podium and give her a pearl necklace and I got paid a hundred pounds.'

See Janet pick up the bamboo skewers.

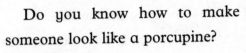

Do you know how to make someone look like a porcupine?

Janet does.

Poor John.

# A Trip to the Charity Shop

Today, John is going to take some old clothes to the charity shop.

Janet says, 'Make sure they don't keep you, John.'

Hear John laugh and laugh.

John picks up the bag of old things from the hall and skips gaily down the road swinging his bag.

When John gets to the shop, Mrs McCarthy is taking down a display of Christmas crackers from the window. See Mrs McCarthy wave at John. What fun!

John tries the shop door, but it is blocked by a big box full of old grandfather clock parts.

Mrs McCarthy shouts to John that he should come around the back.

When John arrives at the back door, Mrs McCarthy says, 'Have you got some nice things for me, John?'

'Yes,' says John. 'I have some old clothes I don't wear any more. There is a nice pair of purple lurex trousers, an aquamarine satin waistcoat, a pair of pink cowboy boots and a green floppy hat with an ostrich feather.'

Do you know how to smile through clenched teeth? Mrs McCarthy does.

'Would you like a hand taking down the Christmas display?' says John.

'Thank you,' says Mrs McCarthy.

Kind John.

After they have taken down the decorations, John sees an old piano and says, 'I haven't seen

 that before, can I have a play please?'

'Of course,' says Mrs McCarthy.

John sits down and plays 'The Lambeth Walk' and 'Mother Kelly's Doorstep'. Clever John.

Soon, it is time for John to leave. He says goodbye to Mrs McCarthy and trots back home, trying not to tread on any of the cracks in the pavement.

When John gets home Janet is making some toasted sandwiches.

'You were gone a long time,' says Janet.

'Yes', says John, 'I saw Mrs McCarthy, I hadn't seen her upright before. So after I helped her take down her crackers, she let me knock out a couple of firm favourites. I'm late because when I finally got in I could only manage to get as far as the old clock weights, so she said I could try the back door.'

Can you get someone's whole head into an electric sandwich toaster?

Janet can.

Smell the burning hair.

Poor John.

# Janet and John Go to London

Today, Janet and John are going to London.

Do you know where London is? John has a part-time job in London.

Janet is going shopping while John goes to work. Janet is very good at shopping. See the credit-card statements.

John dresses in his work clothes – a maroon satin matador outfit with gold trimmings and buckled shoes. Do you know what a popinjay is?

Janet and John arrive at the railway station and buy their tickets.

Soon they are on the train. Janet has to put John's reins on to stop him running up and down making train noises.

When they arrive in London, Janet says to John, 'I'm going to the shops now to get a new umbrella. I'll meet you back here at three o'clock.'

John knows how to tell the time. Clever John.

John waves goodbye to Janet and gets the bus to work.

John has finished his job as a weather-boy by lunchtime, so he goes for a walk.

When John is walking down the road, he sees a sign saying 'Extras wanted – filming here today'.

John knows all about extras. John sees the lady on the desk and says, 'Can I be in your film please?'

The lady says, 'The only part we have left is for a drinks waiter. We can pay you fifty pounds if that's OK?'

'Yes thank you,' says John.

The producer says to John, 'We'd like you to be

the drinks waiter. When the lady signals to you, you must bring a glass of cream sherry to the lady on the couch, then stand at the back with the bottle on the tray. Can you act the part of a waiter?'

John says, 'Yes, I have an Equity card.'

John takes the tray to the lady four times and gives her some sherry. The rest of the time John has to wait at the back of the set with the bottle on a tray.

When the filming has finished John says, 'My arm is very tired now, can I have some sherry please?'

The producer says, 'Yes, but we only have dry sherry left.'

John does not really like dry sherry, but has a big glass anyway.

Soon it is time to meet Janet. See John hop and skip down the road. What fun!

Janet says, 'You're late. What have you been doing?'

John says, 'I've been helping to make a film. They wanted me to stand at the back until I was needed then give the lady laying on the couch some Bristol cream. I had to do it four times and all I got was fifty pounds, and ended up with a tired arm and a dry sack for my trouble.'

Do you know how to ruin a new umbrella?

Janet does.

Poor John.

# John Goes for a Bicycle Ride

Today, John is going for a bicycle ride.

Do you like riding a bicycle? John does.

John has a purple chopper with training wheels.

See John put on his best cycling costume: a bright-green lurex catsuit with a white circle pattern, a shiny red helmet and solid silver cycle clips.

Janet says, 'You look like a bag of frozen Brussels sprouts.'

See John do a cross face.

Janet says, 'Don't be long, lunch will be ready

in half an hour. We're having lasagne.'

John likes lasagne. See John's little pot belly.

See how fast John can ride down to the park.

When John gets to the park, he sees Mrs Sutton.

'Hello Mrs Sutton,' says John.

'Hello John,' says Mrs Sutton.

What fun!

John says, 'I quite often see you in the park when I'm riding my bicycle.'

'Yes,' says Mrs Sutton. 'My husband is making me some furniture and it's a surprise, so I spend quite a lot of time down here. When it's windy, some of the big trees lose branches or even blow down and Mr Sutton often can't get the special wood he needs for turning. I am keeping my eye on that *Sorbus torminalis* as it nearly came down in the last storm and the wood is perfect for what he needs. It's quite a rare tree nowadays. They used to use the fruit for flavouring beer. If you get them when they are very ripe, they taste just like dates.'

Clever Mrs Sutton.

John asks, 'Do you know what Mr Sutton is making?'

Mrs Sutton says, 'I hope it's a tallboy for the front hall, I've wanted one for years.'

John waves goodbye to Mrs Sutton and pedals quickly home, ringing his bell all the way. 'Ding-a-ling'.

When John gets home, Janet is just taking the lasagne out from under the grill.

Janet says, 'Did you have a nice ride, John?'

'Yes,' says John. 'I saw Mrs Sutton in the park. She said she spends a lot of time down there looking out for a wild service because her husband has trouble getting wood. She said that if she waited around long enough, she might be lucky and get a tallboy in her front entrance.'

See Janet tip hot lasagne down John's tights.

Hear the screams.

Poor John.

# A Day at the Beach

Today, it is a lovely day and Janet and John are going to the beach.

John puts on his special sparkly, pink swimming costume with matching cape, flippers and snorkel.

See Janet packing some sandwiches, fizzy drink, cakes and a big box of beard-wipes in a hamper. What fun!

Soon Janet and John are in the car.

Do you know how many times John can say 'are we there yet' in half an hour? Janet does.

When Janet and John arrive at the beach, it is

quite windy, so Janet hires a windbreak and some deckchairs.

Janet says, 'I'm going to have a walk around the shops, you stay here and try to behave.'

'I will,' says John.

John sees a man with a donkey giving rides on the beach. The donkey is light brown with a dark-brown muzzle. John asks the man what the donkey is called.

Do you think 'Sanchez' is a funny name? John does.

John sees a big sign at the end of the beach that says 'Free ice cream'. John likes ice cream. Do you have a wobbly tummy? John does.

See John hop and skip along the beach to the stall giving away ice cream.

When John gets to the front of the queue he sees a lady with a badge that says 'Mrs Dickinson'.

John says, 'Hello Mrs Dickinson, my name is John and I'd like some ice cream please.'

'Hello John,' says Mrs Dickinson. 'I'm just

about to have some myself as it is time for me to take a break. That is a lovely costume you have there.'

See John blush.

Mrs Dickinson says, 'These ice creams are quite new, they are made from fruit smoothies.'

Do you think 'Jubbly' is a funny name for an ice cream?

John does.

John has quite a lot of trouble getting the wrapper off and drops it in the sand. See John blub.

Mrs Dickinson has almost finished her ice cream, so she gives him a hand to unwrap the ice cream before it is completely melted. Mrs Dickinson wipes the ice cream from her hands and dries John's tears with a tissue.

See John and Mrs Dickinson walk to the end of the pier and listen to someone playing the barrel organ.

Soon it is time to meet Janet. John waves

goodbye to Mrs Dickinson and trots back to the deckchairs.

Soon Janet comes back from the shops. 'You are very messy, John, what have you been up to?'

John says, 'I was walking along the beach and I saw Mrs Dickinson. She was letting people try out her Jubblies on the beach for free. I had trouble getting hold of mine and got it covered in sand, so Mrs Dickinson gave me a hand. It was running over her knuckles by the time she'd sorted it out. Then we went to the end of the pier and enjoyed an organ-grinder.'

See Janet play a game called 'bury the newsreader up to his neck in the sand'.

See the tide coming in.

Poor John.

# At the Grocer's

Today, John is going to the grocer's shop in the village.

John likes to go to the grocer's as he can buy some sweets while he is there.

John likes sweets. Do you know what a muffin-top is?

Janet says, 'I'd like some ham on the bone, some Cheddar and a box of crackers. Can you remember all that, John?'

John says, 'Of course I can.'

Clever John.

Janet says, 'Don't be long, I'll be doing some ironing.'

John puts on his shopping clothes: purple loon-pants with gold stars, a turquoise satin shirt with an orange cravat and a silver top hat with a pink ribbon.

John is a dandy.

See Janet give John the money for the shopping and wave goodbye at the door.

See John hop and skip gaily down the road to the shops.

Soon John arrives at the grocer's. 'Ding-a-ling' goes the shop bell.

John sees Mrs Palmer behind the counter.

'Hello Mrs Palmer,' says John.

'Hello John,' says Mrs Palmer.

What fun!

Mrs Palmer is trying to open a big jar of olives.

Do you like olives? Neither does John.

Mrs Palmer says, 'Sorry to keep you, John, Mr

Palmer normally opens these for me, but he's had to go out. Could you help?'

See John open the jar of olives. See how strong John is.

Mrs Palmer says, 'Thank you, John. I wonder if you could help me with something else?'

John says, 'Of course.'

Kind John.

Mrs Palmer says, 'I can't reach that big box of breakfast cereal on the top shelf, could you get it down for me?'

See John reach up and get down the big box. John likes top shelves.

See how tall John is.

'Thank you very much, John,' says Mrs Palmer. 'What can I get you today?'

John says, 'I'd like some ham on the bone, some Cheddar and a box of crackers please.'

'Certainly,' says Mrs Palmer, 'and because you've been so helpful, you can have a bag of sweets for free.'

While Mrs Palmer is cutting the ham, John looks at all of the jars of sweets.

John says, 'I'd like a bag of raspberry pips please.'

See Mrs Palmer give John the shopping and a bag of sweets.

'Goodbye Mrs Palmer,' says John, as he trots home with his shopping.

When John gets home, Janet has just finished the ironing.

'You took a long time,' says Janet.

'Yes,' says John. 'When I got to the shop, Mr Palmer wasn't there, so Mrs Palmer asked if I could help out with some of the things he does for her. He normally handles olives on a Tuesday, so as he was out, I managed to get the top off and hand down her Shreddies. She was so pleased that she gave me a big bag of sweets for free.'

See Janet tie John to the ironing board.

Can you reduce the appearance
of ageing wrinkles?

Janet can.

Hear the screams.

Poor John.

# The Television Repair

Today, Janet is going to work.

Janet says, 'Don't forget that someone is coming over to fix that old television in the shed.'

John says, 'Don't worry, Janet, I'll be here all day.'

Later that morning there is a ring on the doorbell – 'ding-dong'.

John goes to the door. It is Mrs Walton from the television shop. She says, 'I've come to fix your television, Mr Marsh.'

John takes her up the back passage and shows her the television in the shed.

Mrs Walton says, 'It is rather an old one isn't it?'

'Yes,' says John, 'but it was working fine until last week when the picture went all fuzzy.'

Do you sometimes go all fuzzy? John does.

Mrs Walton says, 'It's probably a bit damp down there. You shouldn't really keep televisions where it's damp.'

Silly John.

'If you could move all those dirty magazines and videos, as I don't want to get dusty, I'll make a start.'

John goes to make Mrs Walton a cup of tea.

When John comes back with the cup of tea, Mrs Walton has finished working on the television. Clever Mrs Walton.

Mrs Walton says, 'While I was here I fixed that old black-and-white television with the fuzzy picture. The aerial needed trimming.'

'Thank you, Mrs Walton,' says John.

When Janet comes home, John is in the shed.

Janet calls out to John, 'Did you get the television repaired?'

John runs in from the shed. 'Yes,' says John. 'Mrs Walton said I couldn't keep my Fidelity in the shed. She soon sorted that out. She tweaked my horizontal hold and afterwards trimmed my old fuzzy black-and-white Bush so I could see it more clearly.'

See Janet boil.

John says, 'What are you doing with the remote control, Janet?'

See John run.

# John Plays in the Garden

Today, John is playing in the garden.

Janet says that John can't get into mischief in the garden. Clever Janet.

Do you know what mischief is? John does. John is an expert. See the bruises.

Janet is going to the shops on her own 'for a bit of peace and quiet'.

'Play nicely,' says Janet.

See John wave to Janet.

After Janet has gone, John sees Mrs Frontage who is next door in her garden.

Janet sometimes says that Mrs Frontage is a trollop. Do you know what a trollop is? John doesn't.

Mrs Frontage has a shop with black windows in the village called 'Private Shop'.

See everything.

'Hello Mrs Frontage,' says John.

'Hello Johnny,' says Mrs Frontage.

What fun!

Melanie Frontage says, 'I have seen you looking through your binoculars every time I go into the garden. Would you like to come around for a proper look?'

'Yes please,' says John.

See John climb over the fence.

'There,' says Mrs Frontage, 'now you can see.'

See John looking at the wild birds in Mrs Frontage's garden.

John says, 'It's a shame we don't have a bird table or bird bath in our garden.'

'I have a spare bird bath behind the shed,' says

Mrs Frontage. 'Would you like it?'

'Yes please,' says John.

Kind Mrs Frontage.

'You must fill it with water and whistle by the hedge to encourage the birds,' says Mrs Frontage.

John picks up the bird bath and carries it back to the garden. John is very strong. See the muscles.

See John clear a space for the bird bath and fill it with water from his watering can. Clever John.

See Janet come back from the shops. 'Have you been good?' says Janet.

John says 'Yes' and tells Janet all about his adventure. 'I was in the garden and Mrs Frontage said she'd seen me, with my binoculars, admiring her ornaments. She said she had one that didn't get used much, and let me have it behind the shed. Then she told me how to attract dirty birds by whistling over the hedge.'

See tufts of white hair flying through the air.

Poor John.

# The Dog Show

Today, Janet and John are going to a dog show.

Do you like dogs? Janet and John do.

The dog show is at the church hall. Janet says, 'Hurry up, John, or we'll be late!'

See John struggle to get into his tight leather trousers and pink frilly shirt.

Can you roll your eyes? Janet can.

Soon Janet and John are ready to leave. See Janet strap John into the car seat and put some saucepans in the back of the car.

When they arrive, there are lots of people with their dogs in the church hall.

Janet is helping with the refreshments. See Janet put on an apron. Janet says, 'While I'm helping with the food, I want you to be a good boy. Do you understand?'

See John nod his head.

John sees Mrs Bickerdyke.

'Eh-up Fluffywhiskers,' says Mrs Bickerdyke.

Mrs Bickerdyke is from Yorkshire. See the dark satanic mills.

Mrs Bickerdyke says, 'Eeee, you're just the man I wanted to see.'

See John look nervous.

'Give me a hand to get some stuff in from the car and I'll buy you an Eccles cake.'

Eccles cakes are John's favourite.

See John helping Mrs Bickerdyke to lift some heavy boxes.

John says, 'I haven't seen that little dog in your car before, is it yours?'

Mrs Bickerdyke says, 'Yes, she's a prize

Schnauzer, I was going to bring her in, but she's a bit nervous.'

When all the boxes are out of the car Mrs Bickerdyke says, 'Right, I need these shifting to the back door of the hall where I'm setting up my stand.'

John says, 'What are you selling, Mrs Bickerdyke?'

Mrs Bickerdyke says, 'I'm selling sparkly coats and fashion accessories for dogs, they're very popular.'

When John and Mrs Bickerdyke have finished setting up the stall, the verger takes some photographs for the parish magazine. John likes having his photograph taken. See the cheesy smile.

Then Mrs Bickerdyke buys John an Eccles cake, which John quickly gobbles down.

After John has had a look at all the dogs, and the sandwiches and tea are served, it is soon time to go home.

Janet and John get back into the car.

Janet says, 'I nearly forgot to bring back my saucepans. Did you have a nice time, John?'

'Yes,' says John. 'Mrs Bickerdyke gave me a treat after she showed me her Schnauzer in the car park, then I did her a favour and took her doggy fashion round the back of the village hall and the verger took some pictures for the church newsletter.'

Do you know how to ruin a perfectly good saucepan?

Janet does.

See the dents.

Poor John.

# At the Optician's

Today, Janet and John are going to the optician's.

Do you know what an optician is? An optician tells you if you need glasses.

John needs glasses. John sat on his glasses and broke them. Silly John!

Janet leaves John at the optician's and goes off to the wool shop. Janet likes knitting. See the unwelcome Christmas presents.

'I'll see you in the wool shop,' says Janet.

See John wave to Janet and go into the optician's.

John sees Mrs Passey. 'Hello Mrs Passey,' says John.

'Hello Mr Marsh,' says Mrs
Passey.

What fun!

John shows Mrs Passey his broken glasses.

Mrs Passey says, 'Don't worry; we'll mend them while you wait. It looks like they'll need new arms. We'll give you some stronger ones that won't break so easily.'

'Thank you,' says John.

See John sit in the chair and wait. While John is waiting he sees a very small tree on the window ledge.

Mrs Passey says, 'Do you like bonsai trees, Mr Marsh?'

'Yes,' says John.

Mrs Passey says, 'I have several more in the office, would you like to see them?'

'Yes please,' says John.

See John looking at the very small trees.

'If you like,' says Mrs Passey, 'you can help me to trim this one. It's a Douglas Fir.'

'Thank you,' says John, 'that would be nice.'

See John trimming the small tree with a pair of scissors.

Are you allowed to use scissors?

'I've had this one since I was fourteen,' says Mrs Passey. 'You've done a very nice job. Thank you, Mr Marsh.'

Soon John's glasses are ready.

'I must get some arms like this for my glasses,' says Mrs Passey.

John gets out his purse and pays for the repair. See the moths.

'Goodbye Mrs Passey,' says John. John sees Janet in the wool shop and meets her at the door.

'Hello Janet,' says John.

Janet says, 'Did you get your glasses repaired?'

'Yes,' says John. 'Mrs Passey told me I have nice strong arms, and while I was there she showed me the little fir she's been growing since she was a teenager. She let me trim it into an interesting shape with some scissors.'

See Janet slam John's head into the wool shop door.

Hear the shop bell ring 'ding-a-ling, ding-a-ling'.

Poor John.

# John Plays a Round

Today, Janet and John are going to the golf club.

Do you know how to play golf? John's friends Terry and Paul do.

See John put on his mauve, checked plus fours, cream silk socks and a purple argyle jumper. Janet and John put their golf clubs in the car and drive to the course.

Janet sees her ladies' playing team and says to John, 'Here's five pounds to spend on lemonade and crisps after you've had your golf practice. I want you to play nicely and I'll see you later.'

See Janet pat John on the head.

John sees Mrs Bickerdyke.

'Eh-up Fluffywhiskers,' says Mrs Bickerdyke.

Mrs Bickerdyke is from Yorkshire. See John Jacobs.

'I see you're practising your swing,' says Mrs Bickerdyke. 'I was going to play with Mrs White from the printer's. She's the only person I know who can play left- or right-handed and still beat me. Perhaps you'd like to join us?'

'Yes please,' says John.

Can you hit a 160-yard tee shot? Mrs Bickerdyke can. See the muscles.

See John line up for his first shot. John's ball goes straight into the bushes. See Tudor Bush get up from the long grass and shake his fist.

Mrs White says, 'I can help you with that. I used to hook the ball dreadfully and that was because I moved my hips around on my backswing. It's called a banana shot.'

See John look confused. John does not see a banana.

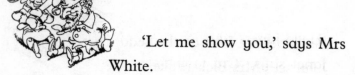

'Let me show you,' says Mrs White.

Soon John is hitting the ball properly.

'Thank you, Mrs White,' says John.

Before too long they have played nine holes. Mrs White is leading, and with her help, John is in second place. Mrs White shows John how to chip the ball out of difficult places and to hit the ball smoothly with his putter.

Mrs Bickerdyke is out of breath. She says, 'I can't manage the next nine holes, I'll see you back at the clubhouse.'

See John and Mrs White wave to Mrs Bickerdyke.

Mrs White teaches John how to miss the bunkers full of sand, how not to get his ball in the water and how to miss the bumpy bits on the fairway. Kind Mrs White.

Soon the round is finished and John waves goodbye to Mrs White and goes back to the clubhouse. John sees Janet outside.

'Hello Janet,' says John.

Janet says, 'Did you have a nice practice, John?'

John nods his head and says, 'I saw Mrs Bickerdyke, she asked if I'd like to join her and Mrs White in a threesome and play a round. Mrs White was ever so good. She taught me all about how to improve my strokes and to straighten out my banana. She used to be a terrible hooker and now she can swing both ways with either hand. We had a difficult lay on the eighth. I asked Mrs Bickerdyke if I could play the back nine, but she was too tired, so I played with Mrs White instead. She was very happy with my length and said that with practice I could make a fine partner.'

Do you know what a ball-washer is?

Janet does.

Hear the screams.

Poor John.

# The Antiques Fair

Today, Janet and John are going to the antique furniture fair.

Do you know what an antique is? Janet does. Janet says she is married to one.

Funny Janet!

Janet and John see the pastor.

'Hello Janet and John,' says Pastor Roach. 'Are you here to buy some antiques?'

'No,' says Janet. 'John likes to help people to repair their furniture. John is very good with his hands, only sometimes he can't get the wood.'

John says, 'Janet has asked if she could have a tallboy next.'

See Pastor Roach pat John on the shoulder.

Pastor Roach says, 'If you want a chat, you have the number.'

Kind Pastor Roach.

Janet sees Mrs Dix, the postlady, and goes to talk to her. John sees his friend Eric from the office. What fun!

Eric wants to know where he can buy some wood. Eric has a spokeshave – see the plasters.

John tells Eric where to go. Kind John.

Next, John sees Melanie Frontage. 'Hello Mrs Frontage,' says John.

'Hello Johnny,' says Melanie Frontage. 'I've just bought this dresser, but it needs some attention, could you have a look?'

See John looking at the dresser.

John says, 'This needs new drawer liners.'

Clever John.

'Do you have something big enough to clamp

them with?' says Mrs Frontage.

'Yes,' says John, 'I do. I can pop around tomorrow.'

'Thank you,' says Mrs Frontage.

John sees Janet. Janet has bought John a new blowlamp for his woodworking.

'Hello Janet,' says John.

'What have you been up to?' says Janet.

See the warning signs.

John says, 'I saw Eric and I gave him some tips. I told him rosewood for fifteen pounds a length, and I had heard that if he saw Mr Jones his hazel was a sure bet for the price of a drink. Then I saw Melanie Frontage. She said that her drawers were coming adrift, so she asked if I'd like to pop around with my workmate.'

Do you know how to light a blowlamp?

Janet does – smell the burning hair.

Poor John.

# John Goes to the Sweet Shop

Today, John is going to spend his pocket money at the sweet shop.

Do you like sweets? John does. See the cavities.

Janet opens her purse and gives John some money. Janet says, 'Straight to the sweet shop now, and no going to that Melanie Frontage's shop on the way back.'

Melanie Frontage has a shop that sells helpful things for people who are married. See the black windows.

'Don't forget to buy your little friend Paul a

birthday card either,' says Janet.

John skips down the road to the sweet shop and opens the door – 'ding-a-ling' goes the bell.

'Hello John,' says Mrs Geddis, 'will you be wanting some rhubarb and custard and a sherbet fountain as usual?'

'Yes please,' says John.

Sherbet fountains are John's favourite – hear the coughing fits.

See John picking out a birthday card for Paul. John chooses one with a man playing golf on the front. Paul likes golf – see the patterned trousers.

'Do you have my magazine in this week?' says John.

Mrs Geddis says, 'I think so, have a look on the shelf.'

See John looking at the magazines.

John sees an article about 'men and their sheds' in one of the out-of-date ladies' magazines. John

likes sheds. See John read the
article, even the long words. Clever
John.

Mrs Geddis says, 'That doesn't look like one of
your magazines, John.'

See John blush.

'I've seen you buying some of the magazines in
Melanie Frontage's shop.'

Paint John's face red. John quickly picks up his
copy of *Organ News*, the sweets and the card, and
pays Mrs Geddis.

See John hop and skip back down the road with
his mouth full of sweets.

When John gets home, Janet is putting some
washing on the line.

'Hello John,' says Janet. 'Did you get your
sweets and magazines, and did you remember to
buy a birthday card?'

'Yes,' says John. 'Mrs Geddis made me blush.
She said that she'd seen me splashing out on
Melanie Frontage's magazines before and this

 morning caught me with my nose in an old *Woman's Realm* at the back of her shop.'

Can you make your whole head go purple?

Janet can.

See Janet peg John on to the line by his beard.

Poor John.

# The Craft Fair

Today, Janet and John are going to the local craft fair.

John wants to buy some new lace for his cuffs and some mother-of-pearl buttons for his silk brocade waistcoat.

Do you know what a dandy is? John does.

When Janet and John arrive at the craft fair Janet says to John, 'Look out for that wool I wanted, here's a piece of it so you can match the colour. I'm going to look for a decent circular needle.'

Janet is very good at handicrafts. Clever Janet.

John sees Mrs Bickerdyke.

'Eh-up Fluffywhiskers,' says Mrs Bickerdyke.

Mrs Bickerdyke is from Yorkshire. See Michael Parkinson.

John says, 'Janet told me I mustn't talk to strange women.'

'That's as well,' says Mrs Bickerdyke. 'I've got to get home to see to t' dinner. Dumplings tonight.'

Next John goes to the wool stall.

'Hello Mr Marsh,' says Mrs Middler.

Mrs Middler knows all about knitting and embroidery.

John says, 'Did you make these cushions? They're lovely!'

Mrs Middler says, 'Yes.'

Clever Mrs Middler.

'I wonder if you have any of this wool?' says John. 'It's a four-ply, one hundred per cent merino.'

'Yes, I think I have some just here. I must say,

you seem to know your stuff when it comes to wool.'

See John blush. John buys the wool and goes to look for Janet.

John sees Janet by the haberdashery stall. Do you know what haberdashery is? Neither does John.

'Hello John,' says Janet. 'Did you get my wool?'

'Yes,' says John. 'I was admiring Mrs Middler's upholstery. She told me that it was a pleasure to meet a man who actually knows something about four-ply. I saw Mrs Bickerdyke but I only said a few words and she had to rush off because she was afraid that if she stood talking to me her dumplings would boil over.'

Do you know how to remove a circular needle from someone's personal regions?

Neither does John.

Poor John.

# John Goes to the Post Office

Today, Janet and John are going to the village post office.

See John put on his postmaster general costume with high boots, a frock coat, a tricorn hat with tassels around the top and a gold cockade. John wants to buy a present for his friend Alan, who is going on holiday to the seaside.

Janet says, 'I'm just going to the supermarket to pick up some lunch, could you manage to go to the post office on your own?'

'Yes,' says John, 'I'll meet you outside in a minute.'

John skips down the road to the post office. See the painted blue pegboard with baby clothes and knitting patterns on it. 'Ding-a-ling' goes the bell.

'Hello John,' says Mrs Dempsey. 'You look very dashing today. I like the braid all down those trousers.'

See John blush. Paint John's face red.

John says, 'I am looking for a holiday present for my friend. But he has a bucket and spade already.'

Mrs Dempsey says, 'What about a nice rubber ring for the beach?'

'Ooh yes!' says John. 'That one over there looks like just the thing.'

See John get out the rubber ring and blow it up. Can you see the pretty stars? John can.

'May I have this one please?' says John. 'I'd like to send it to my friend.'

Mrs Dempsey says, 'Well, we'd better let the air out of it first – we can't post it like this. It has to fit through this letter box-sized slot on the counter, otherwise we have to charge extra for it as an oversized parcel.'

See Mrs Dempsey and John press the air out of the rubber ring. What fun!

Mrs Dempsey wraps up the present in brown paper and ties some string around it. John writes the address on the parcel and a card and Mrs Dempsey puts three stamps on it.

'Thank you, Mrs Dempsey,' says John.

John gets out his purse and pays for the rubber ring and the postage.

Mrs Dempsey says, 'Sorry, Mr Marsh, this is a ten-shilling note.'

Silly John. John pays the right money, says goodbye and skips outside to meet Janet.

'Hello John,' says Janet. 'Did you get what you wanted?'

'Yes, I did,' says John. 'Mrs Dempsey was admiring my trousers. She showed me that she had just what I was looking for and said she'd be

more than happy to handle my
mail package but said that she'd
need to measure it first in case she needed to
charge me extra. She gave me a hand to deflate it
behind the counter and before it went off it needed
three stamps and some hairy string around it.'

Can you force a grown man into a two-wheeled
tartan shopping trolley?

Janet can.

Poor John.

# John Learns How to Be a Journalist

John is not a journalist. John reads the news. Journalists make it up.

John is on a conversion course. Do you know what a conversion course is? A conversion course is something you do when you want to be taken seriously.

John is not taken seriously. People point and laugh. Poor John.

For his homework, John has to have dinner and some wine in a restaurant, and then write all about it. If he writes a nice story, he will get six gold stars. Lucky John.

John's friend Alan knows all about food and wine. Paint Alan's nose red.

Alan suggests a nice restaurant near Waterloo Bridge.

John looks worried.

'What's the matter, John?' says Alan.

John says, 'I have to take someone with me, but I don't know who to ask.'

See John blub.

'There, there,' says Alan. 'I will ask Amanda on reception, I've heard that she will do anything for a nice meal.'

Kind Alan.

John and Amanda go to the restaurant. Do you think 'Oxo' is a funny name for a restaurant?

John is very excited. John likes his food. Amanda is a bit nervous as the restaurant is on the eighth floor and she is afraid of heights.

While they wait to be served John gets Amanda some wine and she soon feels better.

Soon the waiter arrives with the food. John gobbles down his dinner. See Amanda picking bits of food out of her hair.

Soon it is time to go. Amanda does not have enough money to pay for both meals so John makes up the difference. Do you know what a hairy old skinflint is? Amanda does.

When John gets home, Janet asks what he did at work today.

'Today I was behaving like a journalist. I took our receptionist out for a treat. Alan said he wanted Amanda Ryder on the desk in reception because she would do anyone a favour. We went to a very nice place to eat. But Amanda needed a few drinks because she'd never been taken up the Oxo Tower before and was a bit nervous. Afterwards she said that she would suggest it to her boyfriend.'

Can you hit a moving target with a four-slice toaster?

Janet can.
See Janet chase John.
Run, John, run!

# A Visit to the
# Garden Centre

Today, Janet and John are going to the garden centre.

Janet wants to buy a climber to cover up one of John's sheds. Janet says that John's sheds are an eyesore.

See Janet looking at all the flowers. Do you like flowers? Janet does.

John is looking at the garden ornaments.

John is laughing at how funny the big concrete gnomes look with their round bellies and white beards.

John is watching the workmen make the gnomes. See the men tip concrete into the moulds.

See the workmen point at John and laugh. Poor John.

John sees Mrs Perkins from the post office.

'Hello Mrs Perkins,' says John.

'Hello Mr Marsh,' says Mrs Perkins.

What fun!

Mrs Perkins says, 'I am looking for a nice *Thymus serpyllum* for my window box and I wanted to find something to perk up the privet in my front garden. It is very dull in the winter, and I can't seem to find anything here that suits dry soil. I was wondering if I could have a cutting from your *Clematis vitalba*.'

'Of course,' says John. 'I will see if I can find you one.'

Kind John.

Do you know what a clematis is? John does. John has lots of helpful books.

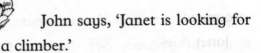 John says, 'Janet is looking for a climber.'

Mrs Perkins says, 'You ought to try *Ipomoea purpurea*, my Doug has a nice reliable one at the back of the woodshed. Get Janet to pop around to see if she wants a cutting.'

'Thank you,' says John.

John walks around looking at the flowers until he sees Janet.

'Hello John,' says Janet. 'Who was that lady I saw you talking to?'

See the warning signs.

John says, 'That was Mrs Perkins from the post office. She was after a wild thyme, and asked if she could have a bit of my Old Man's Beard in her front hedge. She said that in exchange, Mr Perkins has an impressive Morning Glory that you could look at behind the woodshed.'

See Janet push John into one of the big tubs of concrete.

Do you think John looks like a garden

ornament?

    Janet does.

    See Janet waiting for the concrete to set.

    Poor John.

# The Horticultural Show

Today, Janet and John are going to the horticultural show.

Horticultural is a big word isn't it? Do you know what it means? Horticulture is all about growing things. John knows how to grow things. Clever John.

Janet goes to talk to Mrs Harrison from the college.

John sees Mrs Norris. 'Hello Mrs Norris,' says John.

'What a nice display,' says John. 'I can't grow fruit as I have a lot of trouble keeping the birds off of my plums.'

John's friend Reg knows a song about that.

John says, 'Are those Conference pears?'

'Yes,' says Mrs Norris. My Charlie grows these. You can feel that they're a bit firm for eating just now, but they would be nice cooked. Would you like some?'

Kind Mrs Norris.

'Thank you,' says John, 'I'll have them tonight.'

Do you like pears? John does.

Then John sees Mrs Waller.

'Hello Mr Marsh,' says Mrs Waller. 'Are you not exhibiting? Your rocket was the talk of the village last year!'

'No,' says John.

See John blush. Paint John's face red.

Mrs Waller says, 'I have something for you to try, Mr Marsh, it's okra with thyme. Call in on the way home and I'll let you have the recipe, or if you fancy a snack now, I think I have some lettuce here.'

 John says, 'Thank you, Mrs Waller, but I don't want to spoil my dinner.'

Sensible John.

John sees Janet coming back. Janet has bought some new shears.

'Have you been a good boy?' says Janet.

'Yes, of course,' says John. 'I saw Mrs Norris. I told her I was looking for a nice firm pear, so she let me try her Charlie's. I told her that they would do a French tart proud. Then I saw Mrs Waller. She told me I could have wild thyme with Ladies' Fingers if I popped in later, or if I couldn't wait, she'd lettuce behind the stall.'

See Janet get out the shears.

Can you hit twenty miles an hour in two seconds?

John can.

Run, John, run!

# At the Off-Licence

Today, John is going to the village off-licence because Janet has had 'one of those days' at work and has run out of cream sherry.

Janet gives John the money and tells him not to talk to any strange women.

See John skip down the road.

The off-licence is next door to the Hare and Hounds pub.

John is not allowed to go into the pub. Do you know what barred means? John does.

'Ring-ring' goes the shop bell.

See Mrs Davies behind the counter. Mrs Davies

is from Wales. See the consonants.

Mrs Davies is looking for something.

'Hello Mrs Davies,' says John.

'Hello John,' says Mrs Davies.

'Have you lost something?' says John.

'Yes,' says Mrs Davies, 'it's a piece from an old wooden chess set. I can't find it anywhere and it's an antique. I've been looking for weeks. Anyway, what would you like today, John?'

John says, 'I'd like a bottle of dry sherry please.'

See John give Mrs Davies the money and put the change in his pocket.

'Thank you, Mrs Davies,' says John.

See John start to skip home.

John has not gone far when he remembers that he should have asked for cream sherry, not dry. Silly John.

See John run back to the off-licence.

'I'm sorry, Mrs Davies,' says John, 'I asked you for the wrong sherry. Could I have a bottle of cream sherry instead?'

'Of course,' says Mrs Davies.
'Perhaps you can help me? Mrs Bickerdyke
told me that you are very good with your hands.
Could you make me another chess piece? I would
be ever so grateful.'

See Mrs Davies give John a chess piece.

'Yes,' says John, 'I can make one of these.'

John knows what a spokeshave is. Clever John.

John says, 'I don't play chess much, but I do like
a game of cards.'

'So do I,' says Mrs Davies. 'Next time you're
passing, call in for a drink and a game of seven-
card stud in the lounge-bar.'

'Goodbye Mrs Davies,' says John.

'Goodbye John, and thank you,' says Mrs
Davies.

What fun!

John skips home to see Janet. Janet is waiting on
the doorstep. See Janet take two or three big
mouthfuls from the sherry. Thirsty Janet.

'Sorry I was so long,' says John. 'Mrs Davies asked me to copy this pawn for her when she gave me some cream for the dry sack. Mrs Bickerdyke told her that if she was short of a piece, that I had no trouble getting wood, and she said that next time I'm passing I should call in for a drink and poker in the snug.'

See sherry come out of Janet's nose.

Do you know how to pull someone through a letter box by their beard?

Janet does.

Poor John.

# The Eurovision Party

Today, John is going to a Eurovision party.

Do you know what Eurovision is? John's friend Terry does.

Eurovision is a song contest on the television where people dress up, sing silly songs and then vote for the country next door.

Janet says, 'It's time to get ready for the party, John, I'll just have a cup of tea while you change.'

See John put on his best pink lederhosen and a Tyrolean hat with a feather.

Janet sees John.

Can you make tea come out of your nose?

Janet can. Clever Janet.

See Janet wave John goodbye as he skips down the road to the party. When John gets to the party everyone is drinking lemonade and playing party games. What fun!

There is a competition to pick the winner of Eurovision. Everyone has to pick a piece of paper out of a hat. On each piece of paper is written the first letter of one of the names of the countries in the contest. Whoever wins gets a crate of Mateus Rose.

Do you have a friend who will hold your hair back?

Melanie Frontage passes the hat around and everyone takes a piece of paper. When the hat comes to John, there are only two pieces of paper left. Melanie takes one and John takes the other.

Melanie Frontage says, 'I have "G" for Greece, they are one of the favourites. Would you like to swap, John?'

See John shake his head. John is a gentleman.

'I have "F",' says John. 'France has already gone, so I'll have Finland.'

John knows where Finland is. Clever John.

Soon it is time for the song contest.

Melanie Frontage switches on the television and tunes to BBC 1.

Everyone claps and cheers at all of the songs, especially the Germans.

See John hide behind the sofa when the song from Finland comes on.

At the end of the contest, Finland has won and John helps to drink some of the wine.

When John gets home, Janet is waiting.

Do you know what sort of time John calls this? John doesn't.

John says, 'I had a lovely time. We played lots of games and there was a competition. There was only me and Melanie Frontage left. I needed something with a big "F" in front. Someone had already used the French so Melanie offered me the

Greek entry. She said I was a gentleman because I went for the Finnish last.'

Do you know how to lock someone in the coal cellar and storm off to bed?

Janet does.

Poor John.

# John Goes Out to Lunch

Today, John is going to work.

John puts on his work clothes – a turquoise velvet suit with sequins on the lapels, a lilac satin frilly shirt and gold leather cowboy boots.

John works part-time as a traffic announcer on the radio. John knows lots of long words and can even pronounce Welsh place names. Clever John.

Soon it is lunchtime. John finishes work at lunchtime. John fetches a cup of tea to go with his sandwich. As it is a nice day some of the people in the office are going for a drink on a riverboat.

John's friend Alan says, 'Would you like to come

along for a drink, John?'

Alan is a producer. Alan says that producing is very thirsty work.

Janet says John is not allowed to go out with the people from work as they are a bad influence. John says, 'I should probably be off home.'

Do you know any magic words? Alan does. Alan says 'I'm buying' and 'they have a new blonde barmaid'.

Can you eat a sandwich, drink a cup of tea and put your jacket on in two seconds? John can.

When they get to the riverboat there are lots of people drinking beer and wine. See the journalists.

Alan says, 'What will you have, John?'

John says to the barmaid, 'Do you have a Bushmills whiskey?'

John likes Bushmills whiskey.

'Yes,' says the barmaid, 'we have several, but we don't do special whiskeys at this bar. Pop down to the bar at the back of the boat and I'll serve you down there. It's much nicer.'

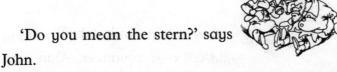

'Do you mean the stern?' says John.

John knows all about boats. See *The Golden Rivet*. At the other bar, they have lots of lovely things to drink and John tries nearly all of them.

Soon it is time to leave. John falls asleep on the train home. When John gets home, Janet is watching the wrestling on television. Janet hears John's key in the lock of the front door.

'Hello John,' says Janet.

See Janet sniff the air.

Janet says, 'Have you been drinking?'

'Yes,' says John, 'some of the people from work were going on a riverboat and I went with them. Alan bought all the drinks. I asked the barmaid, who was a pretty blonde girl, if she had a Blackbush. She said she had and said that if I wanted to have a look at her other specialities we could go somewhere quiet. She said that given the choice she preferred it in the stern.'

Do you know how to do a 'head-scissors

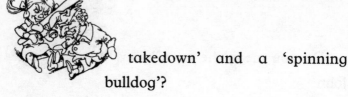

takedown' and a 'spinning bulldog'?

Janet does.

See John submit.

Poor John.

# John Helps Out
in the Library

Today, Janet and John are going to the college.

Janet is going to her first-aid lessons. John is going to the library. John likes going to the library. John even likes the books without pictures.

John sometimes gets books with pictures from Melanie Frontage's special shop with black windows. Do you know what 'shed inhibitions' are?

When Janet and John arrive at the college, Janet says, 'I'll only be an hour, so see if you can stay out of mischief for a change.'

'Yes, I will,' says John.

When John has finished going round and round in the revolving door he is quite dizzy, so he has to sit down. Mrs Mackintosh, the librarian, is standing on a small ladder taking down the plastic letters from the noticeboard behind the desk in reception.

John says, 'Can I help you with anything, Mrs Mackintosh?'

Kind John.

Mrs Mackintosh says, 'I'm just taking down the details of the foundation courses for last term. Would you like to help me sort out and clean these plastic letters?'

'Yes please,' says John, 'but I will have to roll up my sleeves as these lace cuffs would get spoiled if they get dirty.'

John sees Mrs Bickerdyke.

'Eh-up Fluffywhiskers,' says Mrs Bickerdyke.

Mrs Bickerdyke is from Yorkshire. See the ferrets. Mrs Bickerdyke is helping in the college

today too. So is her friend Mrs Gregory.

Mrs Mackintosh says, 'Put the different letters in these plastic cups so they don't get all mixed up.'

Once the letters have been sorted, Mrs Mackintosh says, 'Now we need to give them a quick wash in some soapy water to get them all clean and bright again. Pop into the kitchen with the ladies and it will be done in no time.'

John, Mrs Gregory and Mrs Bickerdyke quickly wash and dry the letters in the kitchen and sort them out afterwards. What fun! Some of the cups have so many letters that they are overflowing. See John write his name with the plastic letters. Clever John.

Soon all the plastic letters have been washed and dried and are ready to be put back on the noticeboard. John sees Janet coming out of her class and skips over to meet her outside.

'Hello Janet,' says John.

Janet says, 'You look pleased with yourself, what have you been up to?'

See the warning signs.

John says, 'When I got here, I saw Mrs Mackintosh up a ladder. She asked me to help her take down last term's foundations as they were due for a wash. Then I saw Mrs Gregory and Mrs Bickerdyke. Mrs Mackintosh said we could all have some fun with the soapy water in the kitchen. The washing took a long time. Mrs Mackintosh only had thirty-four "Cs", which didn't take long, but Mrs Gregory's took ages. You should have seen the size of her "F" and "G" cups. Mrs Bickerdyke's were so full there were a couple of handfuls left over. It took me ages to rinse all the soap off of them.'

Do you know what a tourniquet is?

See Janet make a tourniquet out of John's tie.

Paint John's face purple.

Poor John.

# At the Dog Show

Today, John is going to a dog show.

John would like a dog but Janet won't have poodles in the house. Poor John.

John gets dressed in his orange velvet suit with a frilly white shirt and black silk cravat. See Jonathan Ross.

Janet drops John off in the car. Janet is going to pick up some new golf clubs.

Janet says, 'Be a good boy. I'll pick you up in an hour.'

See John hop and skip into the dog show.

John walks around the show looking at all the

 lovely dogs.

John sees Melanie Frontage.

'Hello Johnny,' says Melanie Frontage. 'I didn't know you liked dogs.'

'Yes,' says John. 'I like them very much. Are those your dogs?'

'Yes they are,' says Mrs Frontage. 'There's nothing like a little furry friend. They're so faithful and devoted. I've even taught them to do some tricks.'

Do you know how to do tricks? John's friend Alan does. See the 'early days of aviation' and the 'flying fox'.

Mrs Frontage says, 'Look at their lovely eyes! Their names are Skipper and Max. Would you like to take them outside for a run around? They're a bit bored in here.'

'Yes please,' says John.

See John take Skipper and Max outside for a nice walk.

When they are quite tired out, John brings the

dogs back to Mrs Frontage.

'Thank you,' says John.

John walks around some more and sees Mrs Moncrieff. 'Hello Mrs Moncrieff,' says John.

What fun!

Mrs Moncrieff is at the top of a stepladder taking down some pictures.

'Would you hold the ladder for me?' says Mrs Moncrieff.

'Of course,' says John.

Kind John.

John holds the ladder while Mrs Moncrieff takes down a big photograph of two boxer dogs.

'That's a nice photo,' says John.

'Yes,' says Mrs Moncrieff. 'Those are Mr Valentine's dogs, last year's winners. I'm just going to put up this year's winner, my dog Benjy. Perhaps you could step back and have a look to see if he can be seen properly?'

'Yes,' says John, 'it looks very nice.'

Soon it is time for John to go. John stands at the

 door and waves goodbye to all of his friends.

John sees Janet's car arrive.

'Hello Janet,' says John.

Janet says, 'Did you behave nicely?'

'Yes,' says John. 'Mrs Moncrieff was standing on top of a ladder. She'd just taken Mr Valentine's boxers down and wanted to know if I could see her schnauzer from where I was standing. Melanie Frontage let me take her pointers out for a nice game round the back of the hall. She said that there's nothing like having a little hairy friend who looks into your eyes and pants.'

See Janet select a nine-iron.

Do you have a powerful backswing?

Janet does.

Run, John, run!

# The Cheese and Wine Party

Today, John is going to a cheese and wine party for the Women's Institute at the village hall.

John has been invited because he is a celebrity. Do you know what a celebrity is?

Last year, the ladies invited John's friend Alan because he likes wine, but he kept falling over. Paint Alan's nose red.

Janet says, 'You'd better hurry up, John, or you will miss the bus.'

See John put on his best lilac top hat and tails,

 with silver shoes and matching handbag. John is a popinjay.

Janet says, 'If you remember, pop into the supermarket and pick up a packet of stuffing for the chicken tonight.'

'I will,' says John. 'Can I have redcurrant jelly with it?'

'I suppose so,' says Janet.

Redcurrant jelly is John's favourite. John sometimes puts it on his cornflakes.

See John hop and skip down the road to the grocery store and pick up a big packet of stuffing, then John catches the bus.

When John arrives at the village hall, there are lots of people there.

John sees Pastor Kidneys.

'Hello John,' says Pastor Kidneys. 'Glad you could make it. We've divided the ladies into four teams, they will be blindfolded and will try different wines and cheeses from each of the four tables. You will be looking after the table by the door and Mr Spicer, Mr Wix and I will take care of the others. When they've finished the tasting they will all vote on which ones they preferred.'

See John stand behind the table and start to pour out glasses of wine and cut up some cheese to put on the biscuits.

Are you allowed to use a sharp knife?

While John is waiting, Mrs Durkin lets John try some Californian Central Valley white wine.

John likes wine, but it does make him go all floppy.

Soon, the ladies arrive for the tasting. John has four bottles of Burgundy wine on his table, and each of the ladies tastes the wine, then tries some of the cheese. Then they go back to their table and vote on what they have tried.

What fun!

Soon, all the ladies have voted, and one of the wines from John's table was the winner and one of his cheeses was the runner-up. Mrs Richardson

 and Mrs Greaves come back for some more cheese.

Soon, the party is over, and John waves goodbye to all his friends.

When John gets home, Janet is preparing the chicken for dinner.

'Did you have a nice time?' says Janet.

John says, 'Yes, very nice, thank you. Before we started, Mrs Durkin let me taste something from the Central Valley. Then all the ladies put on blindfolds and queued up for a sample from each of the men. On the whole, they said they preferred the taste of my Beaune to Mr Spicer's Pinot. Then Mrs Richardson and Mrs Greaves came back because they couldn't wait to get a bit more of my mature blue vein on their crackers.'

Do you know how much stuffing a medium newsreader can take?

Janet does.

Poor John.

# At the Hairdresser's

This morning John is going to the hairdresser's.

Every Wednesday John has his beard curled and tinted and a demi-wave put in his hair.

John says he just likes to look his best for his public. Janet says that it's like being married to Liberace. Do you know who Liberace was? John does. Liberace was John's hero.

When Janet and John arrive at the hairdresser's they are a little early, so John takes his usual seat and waits. Janet goes to the wool shop next door to get some medium-strength elbow patches as she is trying to give up cardigans.

While she is out, Mrs Bickerdyke comes into the salon to make an appointment. Mrs Bickerdyke sees John.

'Eh-up Fluffywhiskers,' she says.

Mrs Bickerdyke is from Yorkshire. See Richard Whiteley.

'Hello Mrs Bickerdyke,' says John.

John sees Mrs Bickerdyke's new car parked outside. It is a small, shiny, red one.

'That's a nice car,' says John.

'Yes,' says Mrs Bickerdyke, 'it's a Mini convertible. I bought it in case we get a summer this year. It's grand with the top down. You must come out for a spin sometime.'

It is time for John's appointment. A new girl is doing John's hair today.

John's new hairdresser is called Donnatella Noboddi, she is from Italy. See the frantic arm gestures. Donnatella has long, curly hair. Do you like curly hair? John does.

John says, 'Do all the girls have curly hair

where you come from?'

Donnatella says 'Yes' and shows John her home on a map.

Donnatella tells John all about her home in Italy and says that she will bring in some Italian food for John next time he is in.

Soon Janet comes back to collect John. On the bus home, John tells Janet all about his morning at the hairdresser's.

'Mrs Bickerdyke came in to make an appointment and showed me her little red Mini. She said I should see her in it with her top down. Then Donnatella was telling me where Italian girls have curly hair and said that next week she will let me have linguine.'

Have you ever fallen down the stairs on the bus?

John falls down the stairs seventeen times on the way home, and it's only three stops.

Poor John.

# On the Pier

Today, John is going out to play the organ.

John likes playing the organ. John is going to a seaside theatre to play the organ at the end of the pier. Clever John.

John puts on his blue silk frock coat with a cream taffeta waistcoat. Do you know what fops and dandies are? Janet does.

Janet drops John off at the end of the pier and says, 'Now then, John. I'm going to the fish market, I don't want you getting into trouble again. Is that clear?'

See John nod his head.

Janet says, 'I'll pick you up here in an hour.'

See John skip down the pier.

When John arrives at the theatre he sees Mrs Ayerst. Mrs Ayerst is going to turn the pages of the music for John while he plays. Kind Mrs Ayerst.

'Hello Mrs Ayerst,' says John.

'Hello Mr Marsh,' says Mrs Ayerst.

What fun!

John says, 'Do you still enjoy the organ?'

Mrs Ayerst says, 'Yes, I do. The Lord Raglan used to have a very impressive one and I used to love sitting on the old pier when I had an afternoon off.'

After John has had a little practice on the organ, there is time for a quick snack and a drink.

John has to hurry with his orange squash as he has chewed the end of the straw. Silly John.

Soon it is time to let the audience into the theatre. See the tartan blankets. John begins to play. Mrs Ayerst is quite short so she has to kneel on the stool to turn the music.

See Mrs Ayerst turn the pages faster and faster.

Soon the performance is over. Hear the audience clap.

'Thank you, Mrs Ayerst,' says John.

See John skip back down the pier. John sees Janet waiting by the end of the pier.

'Did you enjoy that?' says Janet.

'Yes,' says John. 'I gave a wonderful performance and even though Mrs Ayerst was out of breath and on her knees, she still managed to keep up with the fast movements of my Handel and Bach.'

See Janet get a frozen haddock out of her bag.

See John run.

Run, John, run!

# At the Seaside

Today, Janet and John are going to the seaside.

John is very excited. John likes the seaside.

Janet is making bloater-paste sandwiches. John does not like bloater paste. Do you know what dry heaves are? John does.

Soon it is time for Janet and John to catch the bus at the end of the lane. Janet gives John a barley-sugar twist to suck. Janet has to wipe John's beard with a wet hankie. See John wriggle.

When they arrive at the seaside, Janet gives John his bucket and spade, his sandwiches and some money to spend on the pier.

Janet says, 'I am going to the bingo now. I will see you by the candyfloss stall in an hour. If you've been a good boy, you can have some candyfloss.'

Do you like candyfloss? John does.

See John waving Janet goodbye. John skips down to the pier. John likes the pier. See John throw his sandwiches to the seagulls.

Next, John goes to the shellfish stall and buys some winkles. John likes shellfish.

John sees Mrs Bickerdyke. 'Hello Mrs Bickerdyke,' says John.

'Eh-up Fluffywhiskers,' says Mrs Bickerdyke.

Mrs Bickerdyke is from Yorkshire. See Jeremy Clarkson.

'What are you doing here?' says John.

Mrs Bickerdyke says, 'I came down for the American ice-cream tasting, they are trying out some new flavours. Are those winkles any good? I bet they aren't as good as they are down in Devon. They do them hot from the pan with cider vinegar down there. I'll be having some of those next week when I go on holiday. Now I can't stand here listening to you all day, I'm going to pop me flip-flops on and take t' whippet for a walk on the beach.'

Do you know how to get a word in edgeways? John doesn't. John walks down to the beach and makes a big sandcastle.

Soon it is time to go back to meet Janet. See John cross the road and stand by the candyfloss stall. Janet sees John.

'Hello John,' says Janet. 'What have you been doing?'

'Well,' says John, 'I walked down to the pier to look at the stalls and I saw Mrs Bickerdyke. Mrs Bickerdyke had just spent all afternoon tasting Ben and Jerry's. Next week she is going to Devon to get some hot winkles in cider. Then she got her flip-flops out and said it was time to let her whippet out on the beach . . . Can I have some candyfloss now?'

See Janet push John's head into the candyfloss machine and switch it on.

See John go pink and fluffy.

Poor John.

# Janet and John
# Go to the Coast

Today, Janet and John are taking a trip to the coast.

Janet is meeting an old friend. See John putting on his best sailor suit with shiny shoes and fake medals. John is a popinjay.

Once Janet has strapped John into the safety seat and given him a barley sugar for the journey, they set off.

John is very excited and Janet has to change him three times before they arrive.

Janet parks the car by the seafront and says to

John, 'I am going to meet Mrs Dickins for lunch, here's your pocket money and a little extra to buy a sandwich if you are hungry. I'll meet you back here at two o'clock. Try to stay out of trouble today please.'

'I will,' says John.

See John hop and skip down the seafront. Do you like the seaside? John does.

John goes into a sandwich bar near the pavilion to buy some lunch.

John buys a roast pork and redcurrant jelly sandwich and sits outside to eat it.

John sees Mrs Deane. 'Hello Mrs Deane,' says John.

'Hello John,' says Mrs Deane.

Mrs Deane is from Hampshire. See Benny Hill.

Mrs Deane says, 'Are you here for the yacht-racing, John?'

See John shake his head.

John says, 'I don't go racing as Janet says I'd get lost. Do you have a boat, Mrs Deane?'

Mrs Deane says, 'Yes. I have an old eight-metre inshore racing yacht at the marina. My husband used to come out with me, but every time we went out it got foggy, so he doesn't bother now. I am looking for someone to crew for me. I do find that the sheets are a little difficult to handle at times, so if you wanted to do some racing, I could do with a nautical man who knows how to tie off a sheet properly.'

John says, 'I know all about sailing. I have a pretty pink spinnaker on my boat.'

Mrs Deane says, 'I used to use a long, narrow sail called a tallboy, as well as the spinnaker, but I find that the shorter spanker gives me better performance when sailing windward. You would be very welcome to join me for a race, John.'

John says, 'Thank you, that would be very nice.'

Soon it is time to go back to the car to meet Janet.

When John arrives, Janet is waiting.

'Did you have a nice time, John?'

'Yes,' says John, 'I saw Mrs Deane. She was looking for a helping hand as her husband isn't interested as he often took her out into the fog and mist. She used to have a tallboy but said that she was after an experienced man to properly pull down the sheets, spanker and make sure she could be tied up and belayed.'

Do you know how to dance the hornpipe?

Janet does.

Janet is dancing the hornpipe on John.

Poor John.

Part Three
– The Late Years

# Janet and John
# Go into Town

Today, Janet and John are going into town.

John likes going into town as it is an excuse to dress up.

Janet says, 'Hurry up, John, otherwise we will miss the bus.'

See John quickly put on a lilac silk frock coat, black velvet leggings and a gold waistcoat. See John looking at himself in the hall mirror. John is a fop and a dandy.

As soon as John has finished putting on his

 rouge and eyeliner Janet and John walk to the bus stop.

Do you like to go on the bus? John does.

John's friend Alan has a bus. See Reg Varney.

When they arrive in town, Janet says, 'I am going to the butcher's. They have some fresh oxtail in today and I don't want to miss it. Have a look around the shops, and don't get into mischief. I'll see you back here in an hour.'

See John walk down the high street looking at all of the shops.

John stops outside the bookshop. John likes books. See the secret compartment in John's shed.

Do you know what *Spick and Span* is?

Mrs McCarthy sees John through the bookshop window and waves at him.

See John go into the shop. 'Ding-a-ling' goes the shop bell.

'Hello Mrs McCarthy,' says John, 'you look very busy.'

'Yes,' says Mrs McCarthy. 'I am doing some

bookbinding. Would you like to help?'

'Yes please,' says John.

Mrs McCarthy says, 'I am just putting a new cover on a first-edition by Honoré de Balzac. It is quite valuable. Perhaps you could help me glue and stitch in the appendix at the back of the book?'

Do you like playing with glue? John does.

Mrs McCarthy says, 'You have very neat stitching, John.'

'Yes,' says John. 'I make a lot of my own clothes.'

See John do a twirl.

Mrs McCarthy says, 'Now that we've finished that, I can let you have a go at a volume of poems by H. P. Lovecraft and if you'd like to come back again, there's another book of poems by Philip Larkin and a copy of *The Old Curiosity Shop* that needs a tidy-up.'

Soon it is time for John to go and meet Janet. John thanks Mrs McCarthy and waves goodbye.

See John hop and skip along the road to meet Janet.

Soon, John sees Janet. 'Hello Janet,' says John.

Janet says, 'Have you been a good boy, John?'

'Yes,' says John. 'I was just looking in the shop window and I saw Mrs McCarthy and went in to see what she was doing. She said she was rather busy with Mr Hughes's Balzac but she did say that if I fancied it, I could stick the end in. Afterwards, she said I might like to work on Lovecraft and if I got on all right with that we could move on to Larkin and eventually Dickens.'

Can you give someone concussion with a whole oxtail?

Janet can.

Poor John.

# The Vicarage Party

Today, Janet and John are going to a party at the vicarage.

It is Pastor Kidneys' birthday and lots of people have been invited.

John puts on his special party clothes: an orange, sequinned catsuit with a sparkly, pink bolero jacket and matching knee-length boots. John is king of the fops.

Everyone is taking some food with them to the party. Janet has made a birthday cake and bought a card with a picture of the Reverend Ruth Scott on it. See the steaming cassocks.

John has some mature Gorgonzola and some cream crackers. John likes cream crackers. Hear the coughing fits. When Janet and John arrive at the vicarage, Janet sees Pastor Kidneys and wishes him happy birthday.

Janet says, 'I am going to help Mrs Kidneys with the flowers, you make yourself useful and try not to get into trouble.'

'I won't,' says John.

John walks down the garden to where the food is being laid out.

John sees Mrs Parlett from the solicitor's. Mrs Parlett is putting some of the food on trays to offer to people with their drinks.

John says, 'Would you like some help, Mrs Parlett?'

Mrs Parlett says, 'Yes please, John. I see you have some cheese and crackers. Would you put the cheese on one plate and the crackers on another so that people can help themselves?'

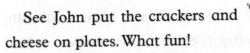

See John put the crackers and cheese on plates. What fun!

Mrs Parlett says, 'I don't have a free hand now so perhaps you could put some of the nice French cheese I bought on a plate and walk around with me with the corned beef and pickle baps I made earlier?'

See John pick up the big tray of baps and the plate of cheese. See how strong John is.

Soon Mrs Parlett and John have handed out all the food, so they go indoors and help with the washing-up. After John has finished the washing-up he hops and skips down the garden to meet Janet. Janet is arranging flowers on the table near the cake.

Janet says, 'Where have you been? I was looking for you everywhere.'

John says, 'I asked Mrs Parlett if there was anything I could do for her. She asked if I could follow her closely with a hard Beaufort and hand round her baps. She had my Jacobs in one hand

*See John Run* 207

and my mature blue vein in the other. It all got very messy so we had to go into the vicarage to clean up.'

See Janet push a big bunch of roses down John's tights.

Hear the screams.

Poor John.

# At the Shoe Shop

Today, Janet and John are going to buy John some new shoes.

John likes shoes. John has 215 pairs of shoes. See Imelda Marcos.

John puts on an aquamarine, crushed-velvet suit with leopard-skin print accessories and a big, floppy hat with a feather. John is a popinjay.

See Janet and John walk down the lane to catch the bus into town.

On the bus, John sees Mrs Cashmore from the village.

John says, 'I have to buy some new shoes today

because I have bought a new boat and I want to get some deck shoes to wear on it.'

See John show Mrs Cashmore a picture of his new boat. Do you think *The Golden Rivet* is a funny name for a boat?

Mrs Cashmore says, 'I once had a sail around the Windward Passage.'

Lucky Mrs Cashmore.

Soon the bus arrives in town and Janet and John start to look in all the shoe shops.

Janet says, 'You are taking an awfully long time, John, I think I will go to the café and wait for you there. Do try to behave this time, my hand still hurts from putting you across my knee in the supermarket last week.'

See John flinch as he waves goodbye to Janet.

In the first shop, John sees some very nice deck shoes and tries them on. See John admiring the new shoes in the mirror for twenty minutes.

Mrs Montague, who works in the shop, says,

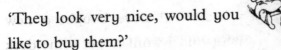

'They look very nice, would you like to buy them?'

'Yes please,' says John, 'but I think the laces have got a bit tangled up.'

While Mrs Montague is on her knees untying John's laces, Mrs Montague says, 'I think you used to come in here a long time ago.'

'Yes,' says John. 'I remember now, you used to have long brown hair.'

'That's right,' laughs Mrs Montague. 'So did you. You used to buy those pixie boots that were fashionable in the eighties. I found some in the stock cupboard the other day that were your size. Did you have felt or leather? I'm sure you'd remember if you saw them. Would you like to come in and have a look?'

'Yes please,' says John.

Kind Mrs Montague. In a few moments Mrs Montague finds the box with the pixie boots in pink leather and John tries them on. They are a perfect fit. John is very excited. See the damp patch.

John pays for both pairs of shoes and skips across to the café to meet Janet.

Janet is sitting at the table with a cup of coffee and a big slice of chocolate cake.

'Hello Janet,' says John.

'Hello John,' says Janet.

What fun!

Janet says, 'Did you manage to find some shoes?'

'Yes,' says John. 'I saw Mrs Montague in the shop and she had just what I was looking for in the stockroom – which was a great relief. Because she was on her knees, I didn't recognise her face at first, but the top of her head looked very familiar. Then she reminded me all about when I used to go into the shop. She said she wanted to show me something I hadn't seen since the eighties. Neither of us could remember if I'd felt uppers before, and the pair she showed me were still in nice condition and a lovely shade of pink. I was so excited I just had to splash out on them too.'

Can you nail someone's jacket to a café table with patisserie forks?

Janet can.

See Janet rub chocolate cake into John's hair.

Poor John.

# John Goes to the
# Fast-food Restaurant

Today, John is going into the village to get some lunch.

Janet says, 'As a special treat, you can have a burger and chips in town for being a good boy lately. I'd like some Ralgex cream too – and remember to pick up some cough medicine, I'm fed up with this throat.'

Do you sometimes have a tickle in the mornings? Janet does.

John puts on some new clothes he has just bought: a Greek evzone's uniform with a white pleated skirt, big sleeves, shiny black shoes with pom-poms and a black hat. John is a fop and a dandy.

See John practise the funny march down the road.

John buys some cough mixture for Janet then goes to the fast-food restaurant to get his burger and chips.

When John arrives at the restaurant he sees Mrs Dickins behind the counter.

'Hello John,' says Mrs Dickins. 'What would you like today?'

'I'd like a quarter-pounder and some chips please,' says John.

'Certainly,' says Mrs Dickins.

Mrs Dickins puts the burger and chips into a paper bag for John.

See lots of schoolchildren come into the restaurant. They start to laugh and point at John.

Poor John.

'Would you like to eat your lunch in the kitchen,

John?' says Mrs Dickins. 'I have some more brown sauce out there too.'

'Yes please,' says John.

John likes brown sauce.

Mrs Dickins shows John to the kitchen and sits him down at the table.

'Make sure you don't get sauce on that nice costume,' she says.

John says, 'It is an evzone's uniform. They are Greek soldiers.'

Mrs Dickins says, 'The pom-poms are very nice. I like Greece. I even enjoy their Eurovision songs. Not many other people do.'

What fun!

After John has eaten his lunch it is time to go home. John marches all the way home.

When he arrives, Janet says, 'Did you have a nice lunch, John?'

'Yes,' says John. 'Some nasty schoolchildren were laughing and pointing. Mrs Dickins said she thought my uniform was very attractive and said it reminded her of Eurovision. She likes Greece and asked if I'd prefer my quarter-pounder in the back. After she'd emptied my bag she was admiring my pom-poms and said that although some people don't like it, she has always rather enjoyed the Greek entry.'

See Janet squeeze a whole tube of Ralgex into John's tights.

Hear the screams.

Poor John.

# John Goes Whisky
# Tasting

Today, Janet and John are going into big town.

'Put something warm on, as it is very cold,' says Janet.

See John put on his yellow fun-fur trousers and jacket and a big floppy hat.

See Janet roll her eyes. Clever Janet.

Janet says, 'You look like a Womble.'

'Thank you,' says John.

Janet and John walk down the road to the bus stop to catch the bus into Uckfield. When the bus comes, Janet has to put on John's reins to stop him running up and down the stairs, making bus noises.

Soon, the bus arrives in Uckfield and Janet and John get off in the high street.

John likes the high street. So many shops and the Christmas lights make John very excited. See the damp patch.

Janet says, 'I'm just going to go to the florist's, you can walk along the high street and look in the shops if you like, but no getting into trouble!'

'I won't,' says John.

John skips along the road until he comes to the wine shop. John is looking at all of the lovely drinks when he sees Mrs Poulton inviting him in.

'Hello Mrs Poulton,' says John.

Mrs Poulton says, 'You are just in time for the whisky tasting, John. Are you allowed to drink whisky?'

John is, but only two or three or he goes all floppy.

John says, 'I used to like a VAT 69.'

 Mrs Poulton says, 'That was a blended whisky, you should try a single malt.'

'Will you join me?' says John.

Mrs Poulton says, 'I've already had several this morning. I started off with a Glen Elgin, which was very smooth, then a small Ladyburn and finally a Mcallans, which is my favourite. Why don't you try these, John? There's a single malt from Scapa, and The Singleton, which is a firm favourite. I'm asking my customers to put down what they think of the whisky on a rating sheet.'

See John drink several glasses of whisky. John puts down the first whisky as 'smoky', the second big whisky as 'sweet' and the third one as 'showaddywaddy'.

Do you know how to go all wobbly at the knees? John does. See John wave unsteadily as he walks down the road to meet Janet.

Soon Janet comes out of the florist's with a big holly wreath for the front door.

'Have you been drinking?' says Janet.

'Yes,' says John. 'I saw Mrs Poulton in the wine shop. She invited me in for a quick sample. She said she didn't care for my usual, the 69, and said that she'd already had a mouthful of Mcallans and was suffering a little from the Ladyburn after she'd had a stiff Glen Elgin earlier. So she stood and watched while I had a quick Singleton, then Scapa.'

See Janet push the holly wreath down John's trousers then chase him down the road.

See John run.

Run, John, run!

# John Goes Sailing

Today is a lovely sunny day, so John is going out for a sail on his boat.

Do you think *The Golden Rivet* is a funny name for a boat?

John puts on his best sailing clothes: a pink blazer with fake medals and gold braid, a white frilly shirt with a blue cravat, blue trousers with a silver stripe down the side and a white peaked cap. John is a popinjay.

Janet wants to go to the fish market, so she gives John a lift to the boatyard. Do you know how to be a nuisance with a telescope? John does.

When they arrive at the boatyard, Janet says, 'I'll pick you up at three o'clock. Don't be late!'

'I won't,' says John, as he waves Janet goodbye.

John sees Mrs Woodrow.

'Hello Mrs Woodrow,' says John. 'Are you going sailing today?'

Mrs Woodrow says, 'Yes. I am just waiting for my husband to bring the tender. Would you like me to take you out to your boat?'

'Yes please,' says John.

Mrs Woodrow says, 'We will have to be careful today because there are a lot of people out on jet skis. The new commodore of the yacht club, Sir Gerald Boyes, calls them "The Romford Navy". I must introduce you to his wife, Marjorie, she has a great interest in church organs. She is quite a busy lady, but she usually has Wednesdays free if you are interested?'

'Yes please,' says John.

Soon Mr Woodrow arrives with the tender and

 takes John out to his boat.

Mrs Woodrow says, 'If you are back by 2.30 we will pick you up as well.'

Kind Mrs Woodrow.

See John sitting on his boat. John does not like to sail too far in case he gets lost, so he goes round and round in the harbour until he gets giddy. Then he gets his telescope out and shouts out things like 'Ahoy' and 'Avast' until he has a sore throat. What fun! When John is quite tired of getting giddy and shouting, he takes his boat back to the mooring and plays with his telescope.

John sees Mrs Woodrow again in her dinghy. Mrs Woodrow shouts to John that Mr Woodrow has put the tender away by the breakwater for the day, but he has asked the harbour master to pick them up in a tug. Mrs Woodrow and John get a lift back to the dock with the harbour master. See John get his telescope out again. John waves goodbye to Mrs Woodrow and the harbour master and hops and skips out to the car park to meet Janet.

Soon Janet arrives in the car.

Janet says, 'Did you have a nice time, John?'

John says, 'Yes. I saw Mrs Woodrow. She was going out for a sail too, but she said she wouldn't mind picking me up on the way back. Mr Woodrow had left her tender down by the groyne so we had to make do with a tug on the way back. She said that I should arrange to meet her on Wednesdays when she has nothing on and told me that if I wanted, she could introduce me to Lady Boyes.'

Do you know how to keelhaul someone on dry land?

Janet does.

Poor John.

# Janet and John
# Go on a Cruise

Today, Janet and John are going on a big ship on the Mediterranean. See Janet and John drive to the airport to catch the plane.

John likes going to the airport, but Janet has to put on his reins to stop him running up and down the escalators.

When the plane lands, Janet and John get a taxi to the dock.

Janet says, 'Hurry up, John, we needed four taxis for all your luggage from the airport and we don't want to be late in case the ship goes without us.'

When Janet and John arrive at
the ship John is very excited. See the
damp patch.

The steward shows them to their cabin. See
John unpack all his bags and put on his best sailor
suit, with blue eyeshadow and a matching bag
with a big anchor. Do you know what a big
anchor looks like? Janet does.

Janet says, 'Why don't you go out for a walk on
deck? But don't get up to mischief! I'm going to sit
by the pool. I'll see you there in an hour.'

See John hop and skip along the promenade
deck.

John sees Mrs Bickerdyke.

'Eh-up Fluffywhiskers,' says Mrs Bickerdyke.

Mrs Bickerdyke is from Yorkshire. See the cloth
caps.

Mrs Bickerdyke says, 'Fancy seeing you here,
John! I'm just going for my half-hour walk on
deck. It doesn't half keep you fit. Would you like to
come along?'

*See John Run* 227

John says, 'I'd really like to, but I get such pains in my knees when I walk for more than ten minutes.'

See Mrs Bickerdyke wave goodbye.

John walks a little further and sees Tudor and Anita Bush. Tudor and Anita are making a film all about people who have lost all of their suitcases on holiday and have nothing to wear.

Tudor says, 'Howdy, John!'

Tudor is from Texas. See the chainsaws.

Anita says, 'You look very smart in your uniform, John. We have a suite with a balcony at the back of the ship. We were just going back for a drink. Would you like to join us?'

'Yes please,' says John.

When they get to the suite, John has a good look around the suite and bounces up and down on the great big bed.

Tudor says, 'What can I get you, John?'

John says, 'I'd like some Baileys with ice and a pink umbrella please.'

See Tudor give John half a pint
of Baileys.

John says, 'I like this cabin. Ours is quite close
to the engine room and doesn't have any
windows.'

Anita says, 'Yes, it's very nice. The cabins at the
back of the ship are much better because it's a
smoother trip. We once had a cabin near the bow
and it was very rough.'

Soon it is time for John to meet Janet. John
waves goodbye to Tudor and Anita and trots up to
the pool deck.

When John arrives, Janet is playing deck quoits
with Mrs Dempsey.

Janet says, 'Did you have a nice time, John?'

'Yes,' says John. 'I saw Mrs Bickerdyke, she
asked if I fancied a bit of a blow on the promenade
deck, but I said I couldn't keep it up for half an
hour, so instead I had a nice drink with Anita and
Tudor Bush in the cabin. She said she liked a man
in uniform. There was a great big bed in the cabin.

Anita said she liked it in the stern as it was a much smoother passage than up front.'

See Janet boil.

Do you know how to hit an elusive newsreader with deck quoits?

Janet does.

See John run.

Run, John, run!

# The Dinner Party

This evening, Janet and John have been invited to a dinner party.

Janet does not like dressing up. John likes dressing up. It is John's favourite thing in the whole world except for redcurrant jelly.

John puts on a silver and black striped dinner jacket, a frilly black shirt and a bright pink bow tie, with a matching ribbon in his beard. See Janet fight for space in front of the mirror. Poor Janet.

When Janet and John arrive at the dinner party, the host, Mr Lomas, gives Janet a glass of sherry and John a glass of Tizer. Mrs Lomas sits everyone down at the table.

See John bang his spoon on the table and rock his chair back and forth. See Janet slap John's legs and hiss. Paint John's knees red.

John is sitting next to Mrs Haywood from the grocer's. Mrs Haywood comes from Stepney in London. Do you know what a cockney is?

John eats everything up except for his cabbage. John won't eat his cabbage even when Janet does 'aeroplanes'. Naughty John.

Mrs Haywood says, 'I don't blame yer for not finishin' yer greens, I don't like 'em neither.'

Can you talk like a cockney? John can't. Hear Dick van Dyke.

Mrs Haywood says, 'I don't go for any of this posh grub. Give me jellied eels or a nice plate of fish and chips any day. I'm goin' outside for a quick fag.'

John asks Janet if he can get down from the table please, and goes outside with Mrs Haywood.

Mrs Haywood says, 'I hear you're a bit of a dab

hand with the old woodwork.'

'Yes,' says John, 'I can turn my hand to most things.'

See Mrs Haywood dig John in the ribs with her elbow and wink.

Mrs Haywood says, 'I've heard that. I got this new kitchen, see, but I didn't like the drawer fronts much so I bought some new ones that match the work surfaces and I was lookin' for someone to fit 'em 'cos my hubby's useless at DIY.'

'I'm sure I could do that,' says John.

'Good boy,' says Mrs Haywood, 'and when you come round, I'll do you a plate of proper grub – pie, mash and liquor.'

See John go back indoors to sit down for the pudding.

Janet says, 'You were gone a long time.'

See the warning signs.

John says, 'I was talking to Mrs Haywood. She told me that Mr Haywood is useless so I said I could pop round and help her fit the new drawers she bought to match her worktop. She said I could have a plate of pie, mash and liquor on the kitchen table.'

See Mrs Lomas serve chocolate and marshmallow fondue.

See Janet reach for a fondue fork.

See John run.

Run, John, run!

# The Car-boot Sale

Today, Janet and John are going to a boot sale.

Janet says, 'It's about time you got rid of some of your old clothes and all that junk you keep in your sheds.'

Can you make your bottom lip tremble? John can.

Janet says, 'We're going to load up the car and see what we can get rid of at the boot sale in the village.'

John sorts out all of the old clothes he hasn't worn for a few years and puts them in plastic bags, then puts all of his old boots and shoes into a big tea chest. Once he has cleared out some of the things he doesn't need from the shed, he puts some of his old records in a box too. Brave John.

When Janet and John get to the boot sale there are lots of people already there.

See John set up the table and the clothes racks and arrange all of his old things so that people can see them.

Janet says, 'I've just seen Mrs Dickins from the village and I need to borrow her garden roller for the front lawn. Be a good boy while I'm gone, and do try to get rid of some of this rubbish.'

'I will,' says John.

Soon there are lots of people at John's stall looking at his bright sparkly clothes and shoes.

John sees Mrs Williams, the lollipop lady.

'Hello John,' says Mrs Williams. 'I will take some of those old tools for my husband and those two vices. He's very keen on DIY. As they are quite heavy I'll pull my car onto the tarmac behind yours and load them up.'

'Thank you, Mrs Williams,' says John. 'I'll give you a hand.'

Then John sees Mrs Smith. Mrs Smith is from Australia. See the broken furniture.

Mrs Smith says, 'I'll have a look at those old records if you don't mind. Do you have many jazz records?'

'Yes,' says John, 'quite a few. Janet doesn't like jazz very much and I have to play them in my shed.'

Mrs Smith says, 'I'll take these Charles Mingus records off your hands for ten pounds. I'm quite a fan of his double-bass playing.'

'Thank you,' says John.

Mrs Smith pays John the money then takes an old rake handle and puts it in the tea chest and ties a piece of string to it. See Mrs Smith play the tea chest bass. Clever Mrs Smith.

Soon John has sold most of his old clothes and shoes and has made over a hundred pounds.

 Clever John.

John sees Janet coming back with the garden roller.

'Hello Janet,' says John.

Janet says, 'You have done well, John. You even managed to sell some of those old tools and records.'

John says, 'Mrs Williams came past and asked if I could help her with some vices in the back of her car, and pulled up on the hardstanding, then Mrs Smith came along and was looking for a bit of Charlie Mingus. She saw that I had a big chest and a long handle and she put her foot on my chest, held on to the end and played it like a double bass.'

Do you know how to put creases in someone's trousers while they are still wearing them?

Janet does.

Hear the screams.

Poor John.

# John Goes to the Boatyard

Today, John is going to the boatyard.

See John put on his admiral's uniform with a frilly shirt, lots of gold braid, medals and a big feathery hat.

Do you know what all the nice girls love? John does.

Janet says, 'Here are your sandwiches, now don't be late for dinner, John.'

'I won't,' says John.

When John gets to the boatyard, he hops and skips over to where his boat, *The Golden Rivet*, is moored and climbs aboard to eat his sandwiches.

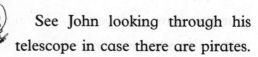

See John looking through his telescope in case there are pirates. John does not see any pirates, so he looks at some birds. John likes birds.

John is looking at the dock and sees Mrs Sibley.

'Hello Mrs Sibley,' says John.

'Hello John,' says Mrs Sibley.

What fun!

See John showing off by winding up some ropes with the winches.

Mrs Sibley says, 'Let me give you a hand with those, John. You seem to be very good with those winches and your boat is very well equipped. Have you ever thought about racing?'

John says, 'Are there lots of prizes?'

'Yes,' says Mrs Sibley, 'there are several big silver cups we compete for every year.'

Do you like big cups? John does.

Mrs Sibley says, 'You should come racing, John. My husband's boat only has two main winches and he is getting a bit old for racing, so with the four you have and your big strong arms, I'm sure we could win some races.'

See John blush.

John says, 'All right, as long as you promise that we won't get lost.'

'I promise,' says Mrs Sibley. 'I'd be happy to look after the wheel if you are worried. Come and see me in the spring when the racing season starts.'

John says, 'Yes, I will. Thank you, Mrs Sibley.'

Soon it is time for John to go home for dinner.

When John gets home, Janet is tidying the shed.

Janet says, 'Did you have a nice time, John?'

'Yes,' says John. 'I was sitting on my boat and I saw Mrs Sibley. She said she'd been admiring the way I handled the tackle. She said that as Mr Sibley was a bit too old for that sort of thing, we should go out together as she was sure we could manage a fast time. She said that she wouldn't mind taking the helm as I have big strong arms

and two winches more than her husband.'

See Janet go purple.

Can you keelhaul someone around a garden shed?

Janet can.

Poor John.

# John Goes to the Bookshop

Today, Janet and John are going into town.

John puts on some new clothes: an electric-blue satin suit with a daffodil-yellow lace shirt and a big floppy hat. John is a fop.

When Janet and John arrive in town, Janet says, 'Why don't you have a look in the shops while I go to pick up a pie for lunch?'

John likes pies – see the elasticated waist.

Janet says, 'I'll see you back here at eleven o'clock. Do try not to get into mischief.'

'I won't,' says John.

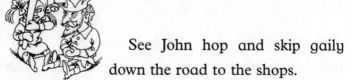 See John hop and skip gaily down the road to the shops.

See John looking in the window of the bookshop at all of the lovely books.

John likes the bookshop window because it has a corner and he can do his Harry Worth impersonation.

While John is waving his arms and legs about, he sees Mrs Wix inside the bookshop. Mrs Wix is from Suffolk. See the tractors.

John wipes the nose marks off of the window with his lace sleeve and goes inside. 'Ding-a-ling' goes the shop bell.

'Hello Mrs Wix,' says John.

'Hello John,' says Mrs Wix.

What fun!

Mrs Wix says, 'Are you looking for anything in particular today, John?'

John says, 'I am looking for some new books because I have scribbled all over the ones I have and drawn beards on all of the pictures

of ladies, so the library won't let me have any more.'

Naughty John.

Do you like ladies with beards?

Mrs Wix says, 'Well, perhaps you need to have more books without pictures in them? Do you read thrillers?'

'Not very often,' says John. 'I sometimes read a Dick Francis on the train to London.'

Mrs Wix says, 'I love going to London, I can visit all of my favourite shoe shops.'

Do you like shoes? Mrs Wix does. See Imelda Marcos.

Mrs Wix says, 'Let me make a suggestion. If you come in every week, I will pick some books for you by a certain author. If you don't like the books I pick, I will let you have the next book at half price. As you like thrillers, I'll start you off with some P. D. James.'

Kind Mrs Wix.

Mrs Wix gives John a list of books and the first

of the ones she has recommended.

John pays Mrs Wix, waves goodbye and skips down the road to meet Janet.

When John arrives, Janet is waiting.

Janet says, 'You were gone a long time, what have you been up to?'

John says, 'I was looking in some windows and I saw Mrs Wix, she invited me in and made some suggestions. She said over the next few weeks I should try something different, starting with *Original Sin*, then the week after that *Devices and Desires* and if I enjoy those she said I could pop around and get out *The Lighthouse* and *Cover Her Face* at half the usual price.'

See Janet rub a meat and potato pie into John's hair.

Poor John.

# Janet and John Go to Tunbridge Wells

Today, Janet and John are going to Tunbridge Wells to do some shopping.

Do you know where Tunbridge Wells is? See the traffic.

Janet used to work in the area and wants to see some old friends.

See John put on an orange satin suit with green piping and a big floppy hat.

See how high Janet can raise her eyebrows. Clever Janet.

Once Janet has strapped John into his safety

seat and given him a barley sugar for the journey, they set off for the long drive.

When they arrive, Janet says, 'Here's some money for your lunch, John, and a little extra for some shopping, but no magazines please. I'll see you in the teashop in the shopping centre at three o'clock.'

See John wave goodbye to Janet and hop and skip down the road to the shops.

John stops outside The Flying Noodle Chinese restaurant. John likes Chinese food.

The restaurant is advertising 'All you can eat for £10'.

John orders everything on the menu from the restaurant owner, Dicky Wang, and says, 'Do you have any redcurrant jelly?'

As soon as John has finished eating, he gets most of the stains off of his clothes and walks to the shops.

John likes shopping. See John go into an art

shop. John likes art. Sometimes he buys special artistic magazines from Melanie Frontage.

'Ding-a-ling' goes the shop bell.

John is looking at all the lovely coloured pencils when he sees Mrs Hudson.

'Hello John,' says Mrs Hudson.

'Hello Mrs Hudson,' says John.

What fun!

Mrs Hudson says, 'I'm looking for some supplies for my husband, he's a draftsman. He can't get the hard HB leads for his pencils where we live, so I have to come here. I've got him a new drawing triangle too.'

John says, 'It's a lovely bright colour. Could you tell me what this swirly-shaped thing is for please?'

Mrs Hudson says, 'That is called a French curve. They are used to join points on a variably curved line. That reminds me, I have to buy him a large one like that while I'm here. He already has the small version. I must get some more erasers too.'

See Mrs Hudson pay for the things she chose and wave goodbye to John.

Soon it is time to meet Janet.

John goes to the shopping centre. When he has finished running up and down the escalators he is quite tired, so he goes to the teashop and orders some tea and cakes.

In a few minutes, Janet arrives.

'Hello John,' says Janet. 'Did you get some lunch?'

'Yes,' says John. 'Then I went into some shops. I saw Mrs Hudson at the back of the shop. She showed me that she'd got a fluorescent triangle and told me that her husband hadn't got any lead in his pencil. She said that he has a small French curve and she was looking for something a bit better, and said that the one I showed her was perfect. Once she'd got some rubbers we were away.'

See Janet rub cakes into John's hair.

Poor John.

# A Walk in the Woods

Today, it is a lovely spring day and Janet and John are going for a walk in the woods.

See John put on his purple and gold walking boots, black trousers with a silver stripe and an orange sequinned jacket with a picture of Lord Reith on the back.

Janet says, 'Hurry up, John, by the time you are ready it will be dark!'

See John switch off his beard straighteners and finish drying his nail varnish. John is a dandy.

When Janet and John arrive at the woods, all the birds are singing and the sun is shining. See

John hop and skip through the spring flowers.

Do you know how to caper? John does.

Janet sees Mrs Ware from the village.

Janet says, 'I want to sort out some arrangements for the spring fete in the village, so why don't you go to the woods and play? I'll see you back here in half an hour. Do try to behave.'

'I will,' says John.

John trots down his favourite path in the woods to where he has made a nice den. See John picking wild flowers and mushrooms. What fun!

Soon John hears someone coming along the path.

'Hello John,' says Mrs Newman.

'Hello Mrs Newman,' says John.

Mrs Newman says, 'I see you've been gathering wild mushrooms.'

'Yes, I have,' says John, 'but I don't know which ones are safe to eat, and I want to make an omelette.'

Do you like omelettes? John does.

Mrs Newman says, 'The big mushroom you have there is called a Blewitt, it's very unusual to see them at this time of year, and the other one you have is a Horn of Plenty. They are normally out from May onwards. I was looking for some too. I haven't managed to find any yet. The small one is called a Morel. They only grow near deciduous trees. If you come with me to the stables I will let you have lots of Chanterelles in exchange for that one. Chanterelles are wonderful in an omelette.'

'Thank you,' says John, and follows Mrs Newman back to the stables.

See John gather up a bag full of mushrooms, then wave goodbye to Mrs Newman and skip back to see Janet.

Janet says, 'Did you behave, John?'

'Yes,' says John. 'I was playing in my den and I saw Mrs Newman. She wanted a look at my little mushroom and said I was very lucky as she hadn't got any Morels. She was very surprised to see my Horn of Plenty and Blewitt, and let me have a couple of big handfuls of her Chanterelles behind the stables.'

See Janet push John into a big muddy puddle.

See John blub.

Poor John.

# John ~~Goes~~ to the ~~Gym~~

Today, John is going to the gym.

Do you know what a New Year's resolution is? John does. See John's round belly.

John puts on his sparkly orange tights, with an aquamarine leotard and matching cape and gloves. John is a fop and a dandy.

Janet says, 'Don't be late for the gym, John, you know you have to be there by ten o'clock before the classes start. I'll give you a lift to the leisure centre and pick you up afterwards.'

Kind Janet.

When they arrive at the leisure centre, Janet

says, 'I'll pick you up later.'

John waves goodbye to Janet and hops and skips to the gymnasium with his gold sports bag on his arm.

John walks through to the gymnasium and sees lots of people warming up before the exercise classes start.

John sees Melanie Frontage.

'Hello Johnny,' says Melanie Frontage.

Mrs Frontage has a private shop with black windows. See everything.

Melanie Frontage says, 'You'll enjoy the classes, John. We do half an hour of aerobics, then half an hour of weights and exercise machines, then spend ten minutes stretching.'

See John look worried.

'Don't worry,' says Melanie Frontage, 'as you are only a beginner, we will take it quite easy on you. I've been coming to classes for some time. If you want to wait for a few minutes after class, you can watch me doing some weightlifting. I am quite good at the clean and jerk now and the instructor says that I'm probably ready to try the snatch.'

After John has been on the exercise bicycle, the rowing machine and the cross-trainer, he is very tired and hot. Paint John's face red.

After a little rest, Melanie Frontage helps John with the resistance machines on a low setting, then John does some exercises with some small dumbells and a medicine ball.

Soon it is time to go. John gets out his Super Matey shower gel, his pink shower cap with the ducks on it and his My Little Pony towel and has a shower.

When John has finished blow-drying his hair he walks slowly outside. Janet is waiting in the car.

Janet says, 'Did you have a nice time, John?'

John says, 'I was very tired, and Melanie Frontage let me have a couple of tips before the class started. She said she would show me some very good floor exercises. She didn't give me very much resistance, but I was quite hot and floppy afterwards. Melanie said that if I wanted to hang around after class, I could see her snatch.'

Can you 'overhead press' a fully grown traffic-boy?

Janet can.

See Janet put John upside down in the litter bin. Poor John.

# At the Greengrocer's

Today, John is going to the greengrocer's.

Janet wants John to pick up some parsnips for dinner.

Do you like parsnips? John doesn't. John sometimes hides them in his pockets when Janet isn't looking.

Janet says, 'Wrap up warm, John, it is quite cold today.'

John puts on pink leather trousers with knee-high white platform boots and an imitation tiger-fur coat with orange satin piping. John is a dandy.

Janet gives John the money for the parsnips and

 reminds John to be careful crossing the road.

Do you know the Green Cross Code? John does. Clever John.

When John arrives at the greengrocer's he sees Mrs Snape.

'Hello Mrs Snape,' says John.

Mrs Snape says, 'What can I get for you today, John?'

John says, 'I'd like some parsnips please.'

Mrs Snape says, 'You don't really like parsnips do you, John?'

See John shake his head.

Mrs Snape says, 'That's all right, neither do I. But I do have some new fruits in that Mrs Hudson is trying out in a fruit salad. Would you like some?'

'Yes please,' says John.

Mrs Snape takes John through to the kitchen where Mrs Hudson is making the fruit salad.

Mrs Hudson says, 'I'm trying to use lots of

different apples in this one. I do prefer the local Orange Pippin that Mr Snape sells, but I have made this one with two varieties called Liberty and Temptation.'

John says, 'What are the other fruits please?'

Mrs Snape says, 'Lychees, passion fruit and some Indian pears.'

John says, 'I like that last one very much.'

Mrs Snape says, 'I will let you have one to try at home. It's actually a type of cactus.'

Kind Mrs Snape.

When John gets home, Janet says, 'Did you get the parsnips, John?'

'Yes,' says John. 'While I was there Mrs Snape invited me into the kitchen to try something with her and Mrs Hudson. Mrs Hudson took a bit of a Liberty with a Temptation and told me that although it was nice to try something new she is happy with what Mr Snape gives her as she prefers local Cox. I had a very nice time and came back with a prickly pear.'

See Janet pick up a very big
parsnip.

See John run.

Run, John, run!

# Janet and John Go to a Flower Show

Today, Janet and John are going to an autumn flower show in the village.

Do you like autumn flowers?

John puts on his pink flower-print dungarees and sparkly gold wellington boots. John is a fop.

The flower show is being held in a big tent on the vicarage lawn. When Janet and John arrive, Janet sees Pastor Kidneys.

Janet says, 'I'm just going to talk to Pastor Kidneys about the harvest festival. Can I trust you not to get into mischief, John?'

See John nod his head and do a special 'newsreaders' honour' sign with two fingers.

John walks around the show looking at all the lovely autumn flowers.

John sees Mrs De Feu putting out a display with some very nice pink flowers.

'Hello John,' says Mrs De Feu.

Mrs De Feu is from Guernsey. See the worried bankers.

John says, 'Those are very pretty flowers.'

Mrs De Feu says, 'They are called Colchicum. They are quite like crocuses, but flower in the autumn instead of the spring. I have some pictures here of some of the other varieties I have grown.'

John says, 'They are very pretty. Thank you.'

John sees Mrs Andrew struggling with a big wooden barrel.

John says, 'Can I help you with that, Mrs Andrew?'

Kind John.

'Yes please,' says Mrs Andrew. 'I'm trying to see if it has a hole at the bottom for a tap, but I can't tip it over.'

See John tip up the barrel. See how strong John is.

Do you know what a truss is?

Mrs Andrew says, 'Oh dear, there is no hole for the tap. I have the right drill bit in the back of my car, but I am not very good with DIY, can you help, John?'

'Certainly,' says John, and goes with Mrs Andrew to fetch the drill bit with a saw attachment.

Mrs Andrew says, 'Sorry, it's a bit of a mess in the boot and the toolbag is right at the back. You have longer arms than me, so I'll hold the boot lid for you.'

Soon John has found the special drill bit and makes a lovely neat hole in the barrel. Clever John.

See John hop and skip back to meet Janet.

Janet has just finished talking to Pastor

Kidneys.

'Hello Janet,' says John.

Janet says, 'Pastor Kidneys has given me a big bunch of his prize carrots. Have you been a good boy?'

'Yes,' says John. 'First I saw Mrs De Feu. She was showing me some lovely pictures of her Naked Ladies, then I saw Mrs Andrew. She said she needed some help as she had a big butt that needed drilling, so I went with her to her car for a special bit. It was a bit of a stretch, but I had a reach around and we soon came back with her hole saw.'

See Janet go purple and get out the carrots from her bag.

Do you know that carrots are good for your eyes?

Carrots are not good for John's eyes.

See John's eyes water.

Poor John.

# Janet and John Go to the Market

John likes going to the market, as there is a big stall that sells all of John's favourite sweets.

Do you like sweets? John does. See the muffin-top.

Janet says, 'Hurry up now, John, otherwise we will miss the bus.'

John has to rush out of the house without false eyelashes and with no mascara.

The market is very busy today and Janet has a lot of things to buy.

Janet says, 'Why don't you look around the

stalls while I'm shopping and I'll see you back at the bus stop in half an hour? And do try to behave.'

'I will,' says John.

See John hop and skip gaily around the market. John stops at the fish stall, which is very busy.

'Hello John,' says Mrs Abercrombie.

John says, 'You look very busy today.'

Mrs Abercrombie says, 'Yes I am. The man who usually helps me is on holiday.'

John says, 'Can I help you for an hour?'

Kind John.

'That would be a great help,' says Mrs Abercrombie. 'Are you sure you don't mind?'

'Not at all,' says John.

See John put on a white fishmonger's coat and hat and wellington boots.

Mrs Abercrombie shows John how to fillet the fish and display them on the beds of ice.

Can you shout like a market trader? John can. John has a very loud voice that he uses for reading

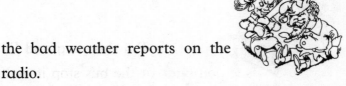

the bad weather reports on the radio.

Soon nearly all the fish have been sold. There is only one snapper left. Mrs Abercrombie is very pleased and gives John ten pounds to spend on sweets.

John buys lots of sweets and hops and skips back to meet Janet at the bus stop.

Soon Janet arrives carrying some groceries and a big bag of chicken drumsticks.

Janet says, 'Where did you get the money to buy all those sweets?'

John says, 'I saw Mrs Abercrombie who told me that the man who usually helps her out was away, so she asked if I could fillet for her. She showed me how she likes the bed arranged. She gave me ten pounds and I left her with a big smile and a red snapper.'

Do you know how many chicken drumsticks you can fit into a traffic-boy?

Janet does.

Poor John.

# John Goes Birdwatching

Today, John is going birdwatching.

Do you know what birding is? John does.

John likes birds but has trouble keeping them off of his plums.

John puts on his best birding outfit: a green waxed-cotton catsuit, thigh-length rubber boots and green eyeshadow.

Janet drops John off at the train station, ties a label on his duffel coat and tells him to behave.

When John arrives at the farm in Devon there are a lot of birdwatchers already there. See the beards.

John sees Mr Oddie.

Mr Oddie is a famous wildlife expert. He introduces John to Kate Humble.

Do you know what middle-aged men think about? Miss Humble does. See the postbags.

John says, 'Thank you for the invitation, I really enjoy birding. I have some binoculars and I know all of the collective terms: a bevy of larks, a parliament of owls and a gallon of petrels.'

See Miss Humble back away, smiling and nodding.

Miss Humble says, 'Why don't you pop along to the hide and have a look at one of the nest sites? There is a group already there, just ask for Mrs Smalls, the RSPB inspector.'

'Thank you,' says John.

See John hop and skip down the path to the hide, which is hidden in the bushes.

When John arrives, Mrs Smalls is showing a group of other children a greenfinch nest.

'Hello Mrs Smalls,' says John. 'What kind of

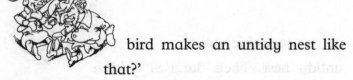 bird makes an untidy nest like that?'

Mrs Smalls tells John all about the greenfinch. Mrs Smalls is from Cornwall. See the caravans.

John sees a badge with a black bird on it on Mrs Smalls' jacket.

'Is that a crow?' says John.

Mrs Smalls says, 'No, that's called a chough. It is a member of the crow family. They are quite rare. I have a picture of one here. Can you see that it has a bright-red beak?'

'Yes,' says John. 'It's very nice.'

Soon it is time to get the train home. John is very tired.

When John gets home Janet says, 'Did you have a nice day today?'

'Yes,' says John. 'When I got to the farm I saw Mr Oddie; he introduced me to Kate Humble, who was very nice. She said I should go into the hide to Inspector Smalls. The camouflage material was quite nice and the hole in the front allowed me to get a good picture of a rather untidy nest. Then the RSPB lady showed me what a Cornish chough looks like too.'

Can you dismember your prey using just your claws?

Janet can.

See John run.

Run, John, run!

Part Four

– Further Adventures

# John Goes to a Cafe

Today, John is at work. John has a part-time job reading things out on the radio for money.

Do you like money? John does.

John spends nearly all of his money on clothes made out of silk, satin and lace.

John is a fop.

John is going to a cafe for lunch before he goes home. John likes to eat cakes, buns, sandwiches and sweets. See John's funny round belly.

See John hop and skip along the road to the cafe.

'Hello John,' says Mrs Clouston. Mrs Clouston

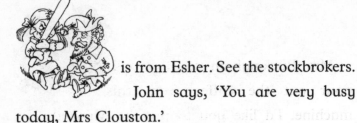 is from Esher. See the stockbrokers.

John says, 'You are very busy today, Mrs Clouston.'

Mrs Clouston says, 'Yes. Mr Clouston is off playing golf again. It's only me and Mrs Buckingham here today and we are rushed off our feet.'

Poor Mrs Clouston.

John says, 'I have finished work for the day – would you like a hand?'

'Yes, please,' says Mrs Clouston.

Kind John.

Mrs Clouston says, 'You'd better put on an apron, otherwise that silk brocade frock coat will get very dirty.' See John spend ten minutes finding an apron that 'goes'.

See Mrs Buckingham get some mugs ready to make hot drinks.

John says, 'I like these coffee mugs. The yellow and black stripes are very pretty. They look like lovely buzzy bees. I have some socks like that.'

Mrs Buckingham says, 'I will pour out the coffee from this machine. I'd like you to put the whipped cream on the top for me, please.'

Do you like whipped cream?

See John putting cream on top of the mugs and helping Mrs Clouston serve the cakes.

Soon lunchtime is over, and Mrs Clouston thanks John for all his help and gives him a big mug of chocolate and as much gâteau as he can eat.

See John wave goodbye to the ladies as he goes to catch the train home.

When John gets home, Janet is cleaning out the freezer.

Janet says, 'You're late today, John.'

John says, 'Yes. I popped out to get some lunch, and saw Mrs Clouston and Mrs Buckingham. Mr Clouston was out and they were both looking forward to getting their feet up so I took his place. Mrs Buckingham unhooked and warmed up a pair of bee cups, then held them out while I put whipped cream on them, and afterwards Mrs Clouston let me have as much of her Black Forest as I could eat at one sitting.'

Do you know how to make steam come out of your ears?

Janet does.

See Janet shut John's head in the freezer door. Hear the screams.

Poor John.

# The Country Show

Today, it is a lovely sunny day and Janet and John are going to a country show.

See John put on his pink and orange tweed plus fours, with yellow socks, black and pink brogues, a bright yellow sleeveless jumper and a white shirt with a purple tie. See The Open.

Janet says, 'Hurry up, John, otherwise the queue for the car park will be enormous.'

See John hop and skip out to the car.

As it is a long drive, see Janet pack some spare pull-ups, and John's best 'Dora the Explorer' potty.

When Janet and John arrive at the country

 show, Janet parks the car in a big meadow and puts on John's reins to stop him running around near the tractors.

Can you make a noise like a tractor? John can't.

Janet says, 'I'm going to get in the queue for the hog roast. Why don't you go to look at some of the livestock displays? I'll see you back here in half an hour.'

See John wave to Janet as he hops and skips gaily to the big marquees to look at all the animals.

In the first tent, John sees lots of goats. See John laugh at a goat called Snowy and how silly she looks with her long white whiskers.

In the next tent, there are lots of chickens and ducks and caged birds. John likes birds, but they often go after his plums.

John sees Mrs Bradley.

'Hello John,' says Mrs Bradley.

John says, 'Hello Mrs Bradley. What are all these birds here for today?'

Mrs Bradley says, 'They are in a competition to

win prizes for the best of breed and
best in show. I am showing some of
my bantams. I breed a variety called the
Silkie, they are in the cage behind me. If you climb
under the table you can see them up close. They
are next to my Sussex pullet.'

John says, 'Thank you, Mrs Bradley, they are
very nice.'

See John looking at lots of the caged birds –
parakeets, lovebirds and finches.

John sees Mrs Middleton.

'Hello Mrs Middleton,' says John, 'have you put
some of your chickens into the competition too?'

Mrs Middleton says, 'Not today, John. I am one
of the judges. I have just awarded the prizes for the
best caged birds. I gave second place to Mr
Bradley's zebra finches, but Mr Tow the postman's
finches were breathtaking – a dozen of the finest
I've ever seen. They will win the best caged birds
today.

'If you come back a little later, I'll be judging

 the chickens and I think that the Old English Game variety should do very well.'

'Thank you, Mrs Middleton,' says John.

See John skip back to see Janet.

Janet is near the front of the queue for the hog roast. Do you like roast pork? John does.

'Hello John,' says Janet. 'Did you have a nice time?'

'Yes,' says John. 'I saw Mrs Bradley first. She was quite happy to let me duck under the table and look at her Silkies and pullet. Then I saw Mrs Middleton. She was saying that she'd normally let me enjoy the game birds, but Mr Tow had left her quite breathless with his magnificent entry of twelve finches. But she said if I came back later, she rather fancied an Old English Game.'

Can you mount a whole newsreader on a roasting spit? Janet can.

See Janet fetch a big bucket of marinade.

Poor John.

# John Goes to the Corner Shop

Today, John is going to the corner shop.

Janet gives John a list of things to buy, and a nice crisp ten-pound note.

Janet says, 'Don't be too long as I want a hand defrosting the chest freezer.'

See John put the money and the shopping list in his leopard-skin clutch bag and hop and skip down the road to the local shop.

See John stop by the estate agent's office and play funny games with his reflection in the shop window. See Harry Worth.

John calls into the shop and buys some plums, some milk and a box of cereal. On the way out of the shop, John sees Mrs Phizackerley-Sugden.

'Hello Mrs Phizackerley-Sugden,' says John. John is very good at pronouncing long names.

Mrs Phizackerley-Sugden is standing by her car. John sees that the bonnet of the car is up.

John says, 'Have you got some trouble with your car?'

Mrs Phizackerley-Sugden says, 'Yes, I just noticed that the hooter on the car was not working again and I was having a look to see if I could mend it. My husband tried to do it over the weekend, but it's still not working properly.'

John says, 'Let me see if I can fix it for you.' Kind John.

John looks at the electrical connections and gives them all a good wiggle.

John says, 'Try that.'

'Beep-beep!' goes the hooter. What fun.

John says, 'It was just a loose connection.' Clever John.

Mrs Phizackerley-Sugden says, 'Oh, thank you, John. My husband is getting a bit old to fix cars. Would you like me to give you some free advanced driving lessons?'

John says, 'Thank you, but I already have a licence.'

Do you have some points on your licence? John does. See Pitlochry.

Mrs Phizackerley-Sugden says, 'If you pass your advanced driving test, it will reduce the cost of your insurance.'

See John jump into the driving seat and do a racing start. John is a skinflint.

Mrs Phizackerley-Sugden and John drive around the block and do an emergency stop. Mrs Phizackerley-Sugden has to catch some of John's shopping to stop it falling on the floor.

'Very good,' says Mrs Phizackerley-Sugden. 'You are a very good driver, John. Call me if you would

like some more free lessons.'

'I will,' says John.

See John skip and caper all the way home.

When John arrives home, Janet says, 'You were gone a long time, John.'

John says, 'Yes. On the way back from the shops, I saw Mrs Phizackerley-Sugden. She told me that her husband couldn't get the horn working because of his age. When she eventually told me to stop, she had to catch my plums to stop them rolling on the floor. She said I probably pulled out a bit quickly after signalling my intentions, but said that I was very good and she'd be happy to take me out any time.'

Do you know how to do an icy stare? Janet does.

See Janet push John into the freezer and shut the lid.

Poor John.

# John Goes to the Delicatessen

Today, John is going to do some shopping for Janet.

John likes to go shopping, but he always has to have a list as Janet says he is as sharp as a bag of wet mice. Funny Janet.

See John putting on his best shopping clothes: cork-heeled patent leather shoes, pink silk stockings with green brocade knee-breeches, a lilac frock coat, and a hat with a big feather. John is a popinjay.

Janet says, 'I want you to get a loaf of white

bread from the baker, and some cheese for sandwiches from the delicatessen. Here is the list, and some money. Don't take too long as I have my shot-putting lesson this afternoon and I don't want to be late again.'

See John hop and skip down the road to the village.

John picks up a loaf of bread from the baker's, then trots across the road to the delicatessen. 'Ding-a-ling' goes the shop bell.

'Hello John,' says Mrs Dashell.

'Hello Mrs Dashell,' says John. What fun!

Mrs Dashell says, 'What can I do for you today, John?'

John says, 'I want to get some cheese for sandwiches, please.'

Mrs Dashell says, 'Well, you've come to the right place, John, we have lots of different cheeses. My husband is the real expert, but he's away on business. Do you know which one you like best?'

John does not know which cheese to buy. See John blub.

'There, there,' says Mrs Dashell. 'Come and sit down in the office and I will bring you some little pieces of cheese to taste. Then you can tell me which one you like.' Kind Mrs Dashell.

See John try lots of different cheeses. Do you like cheese? John does.

'This Mimolette from Lille is very popular,' says Mrs Dashell. 'You might also like to try this sausage too, John. It's a rough country hunter from France.'

Do you know how to pronounce words carefully. John does.

When John has tried lots of cheese, he buys some for lunch and skips all the way home.

When John arrives home, Janet is getting ready to make the sandwiches. Janet says, 'You were gone a long time.'

'Yes,' says John. 'After I picked up the bread, I saw Mrs Dashell. She said her husband was out of

town and asked if I fancied a little hunter sausage round the back. I had a big mouthful of her Mimolette, and she said that if I wanted to pop back for more at any time, I would be more than welcome.'

See Janet pick up the bread knife.

See John run.